Disney Greatest Love Songs

ISBN 978-1-4950-7185-0

HAL•LEONARD®
7777 W. Bluemound Rd. P.O. Box 13819 Milwaukee, WI 53213

BABY MINE

from DUMBO

Words by NED WASHINGTON
Music by FRANK CHURCHILL

Moderately slow

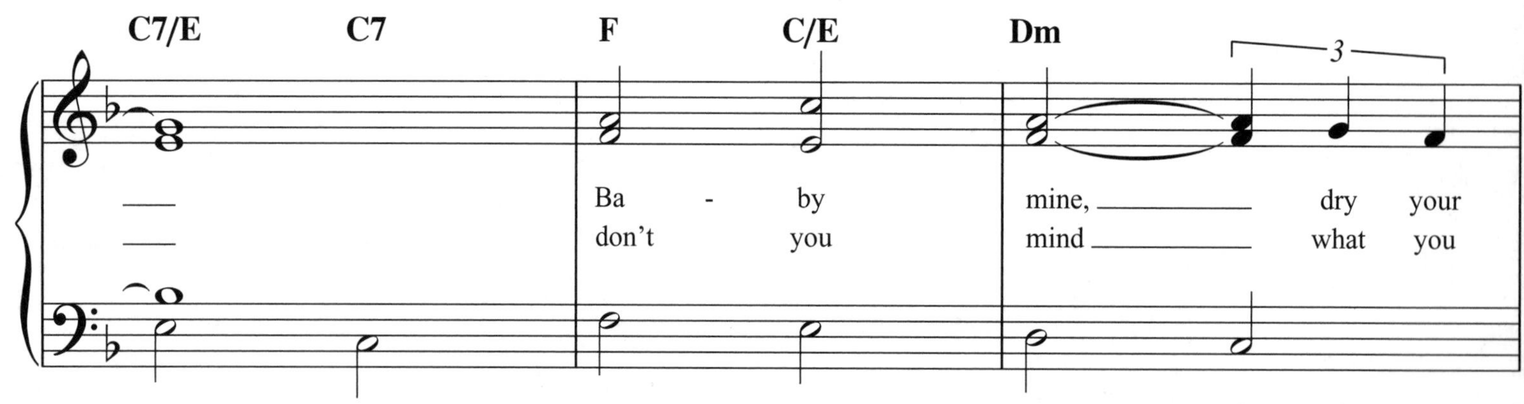

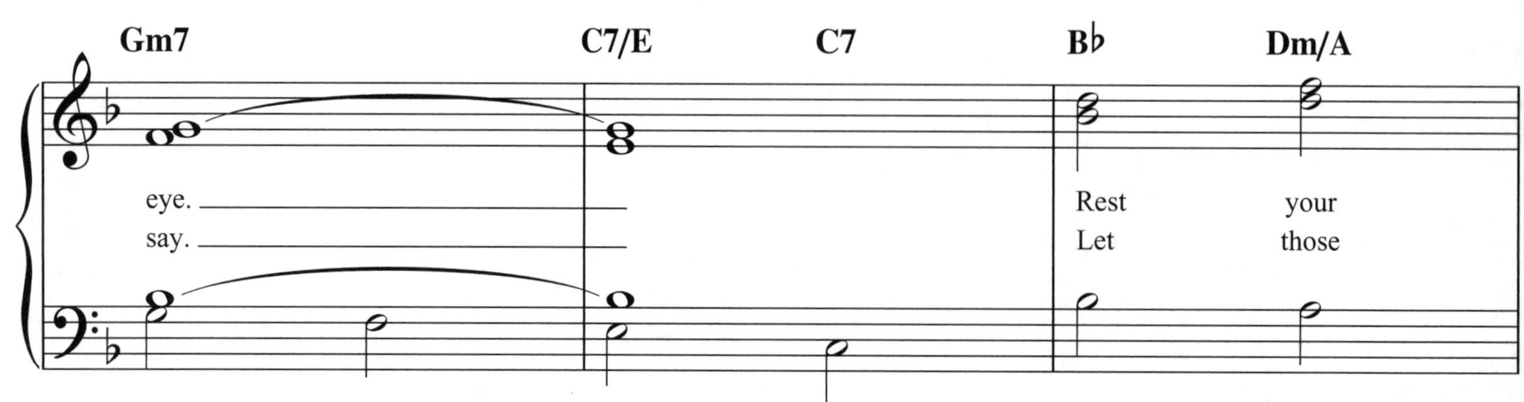

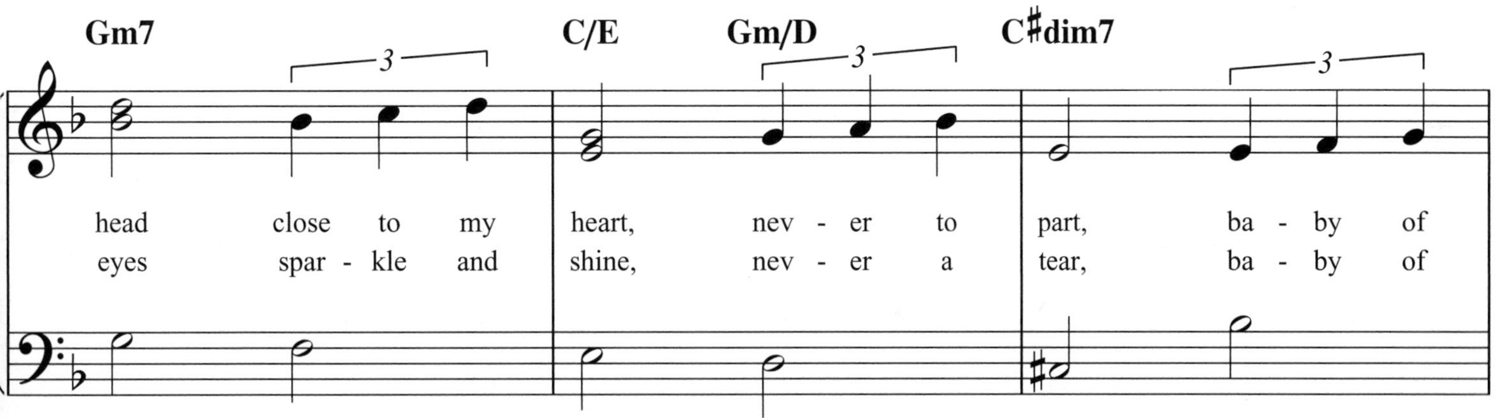
Gm7
C/E
Gm/D
C♯dim7
3
head close to my heart, nev - er to part, ba - by of
eyes spar - kle and shine, nev - er a tear, ba - by of

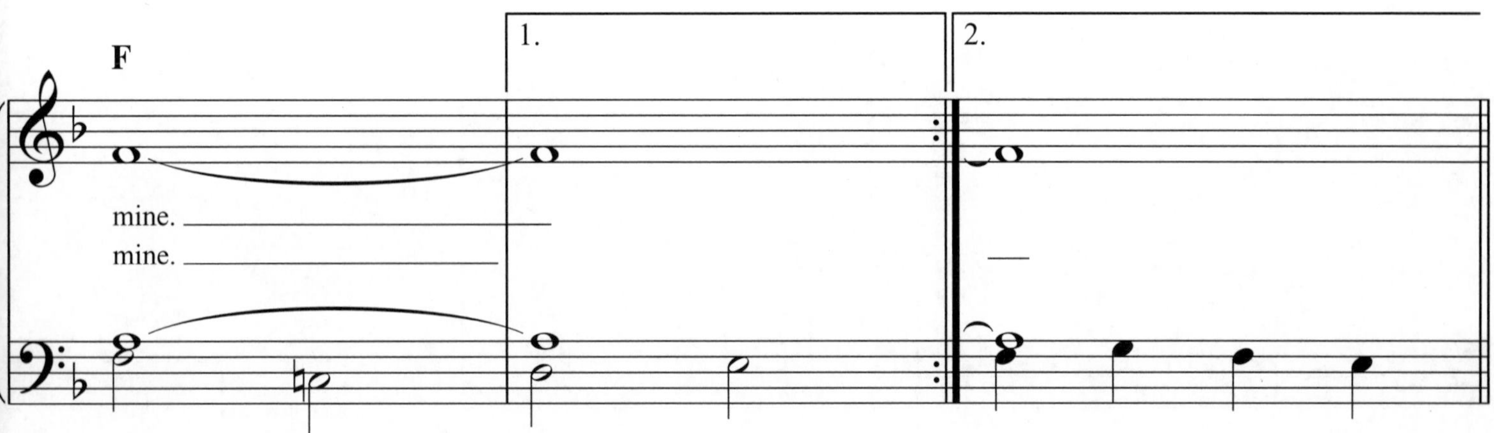
F
1.
2.
mine.
mine.

Slightly faster
Dm
Em7
3
If they knew sweet lit - tle you,

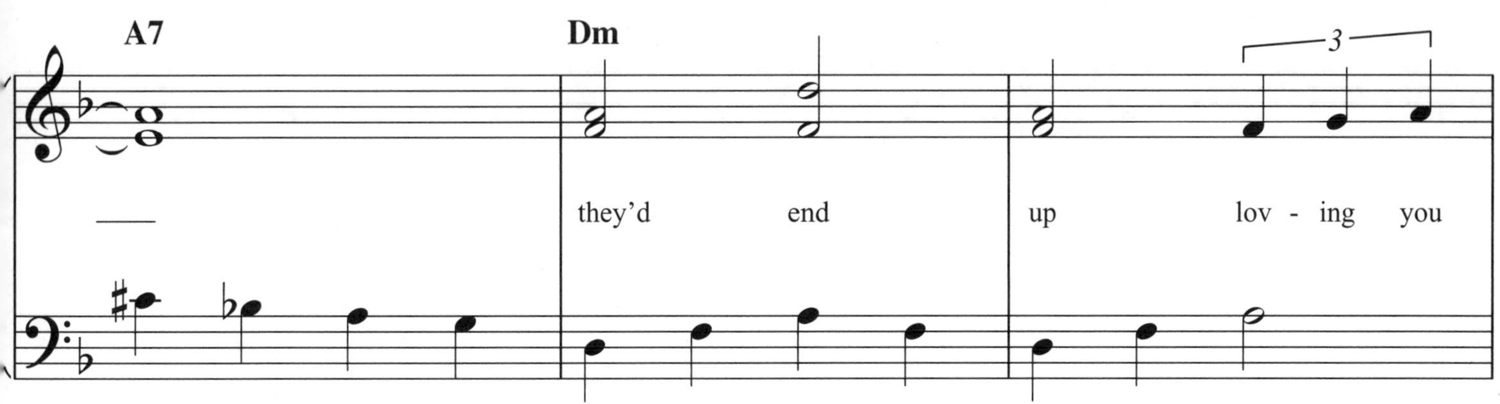
A7
Dm
3
they'd end up lov - ing you

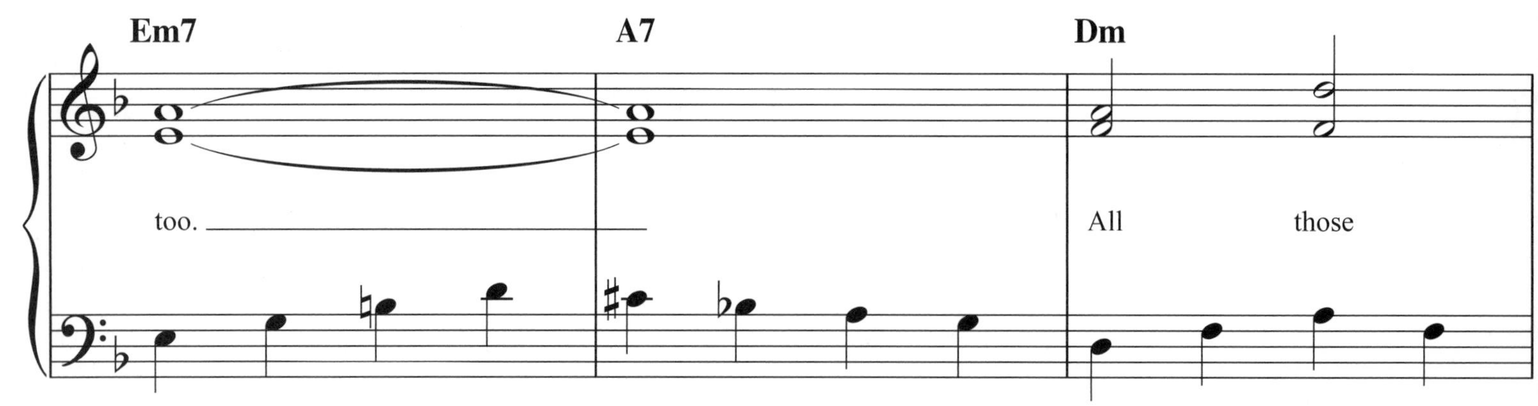
Em7
A7
Dm
too.
All those

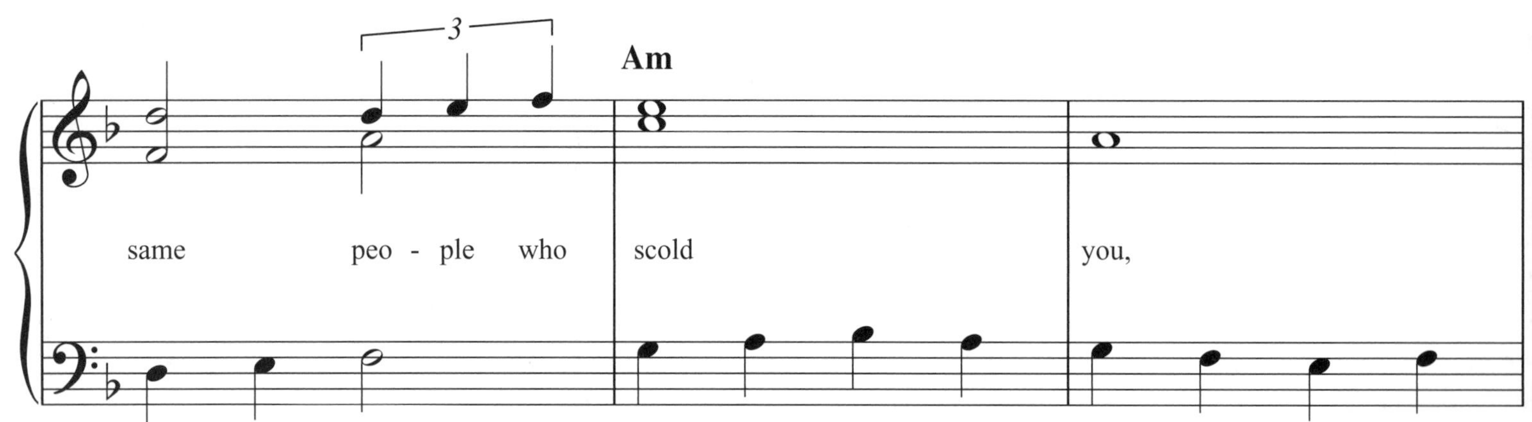
3
Am
same peo - ple who
scold
you,

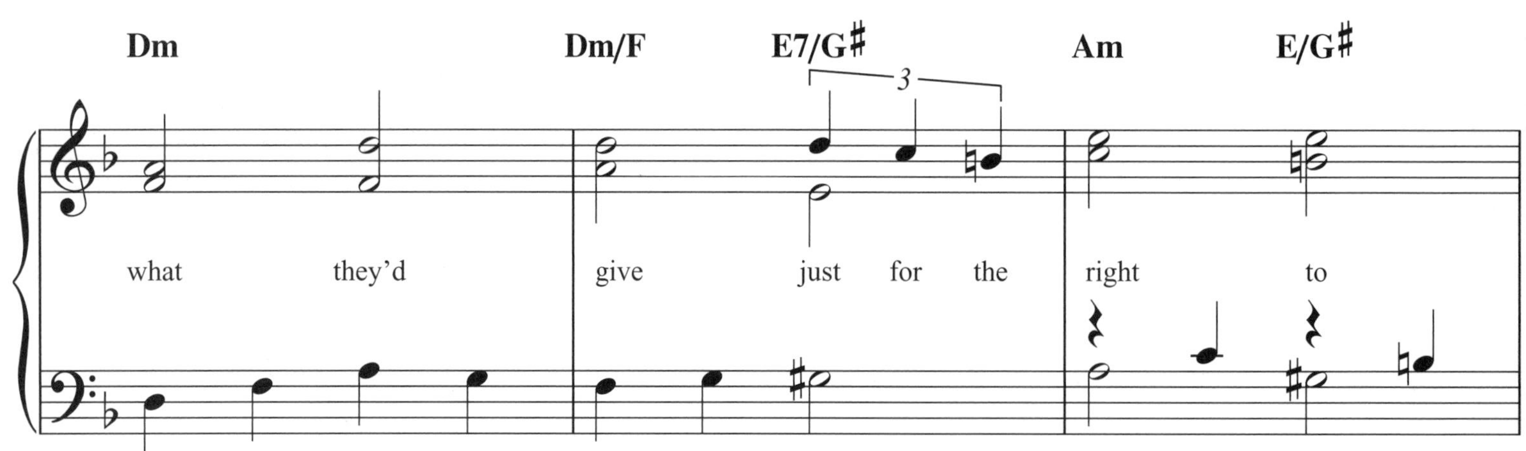
Dm
Dm/F
E7/G♯
Am
E/G♯
3
what they'd
give just for the
right to

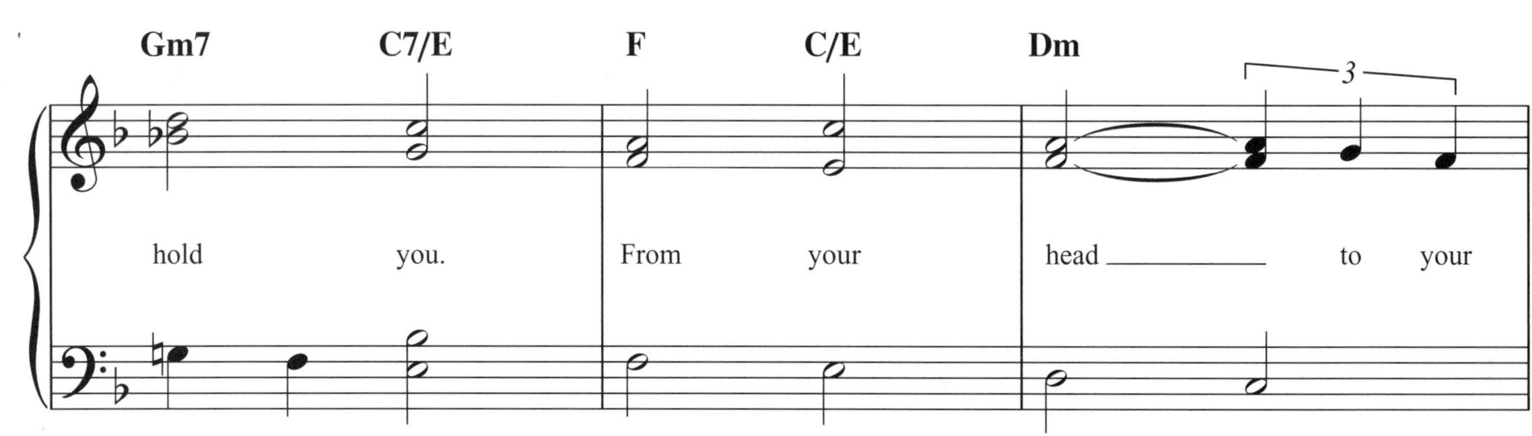
Gm7
C7/E
F
C/E
Dm
3
hold you.
From your
head to your

Gm7
C7/E
C7
F
C/E
toes
you're
not
Dm
3
Gm7
C7/E
C7
much,
good - ness
knows.
B♭
Dm/A
Gm7
3
C/E
Gm/D
3
But
you're
so
pre - cious
to
me,
cute
as
can
C♯dim7
3
F/A
B♭m
F/A
Gm7
F
be,
ba - by
of
mine.
rit.

BEAUTY AND THE BEAST

from BEAUTY AND THE BEAST

Music by ALAN MENKEN
Lyrics by HOWARD ASHMAN

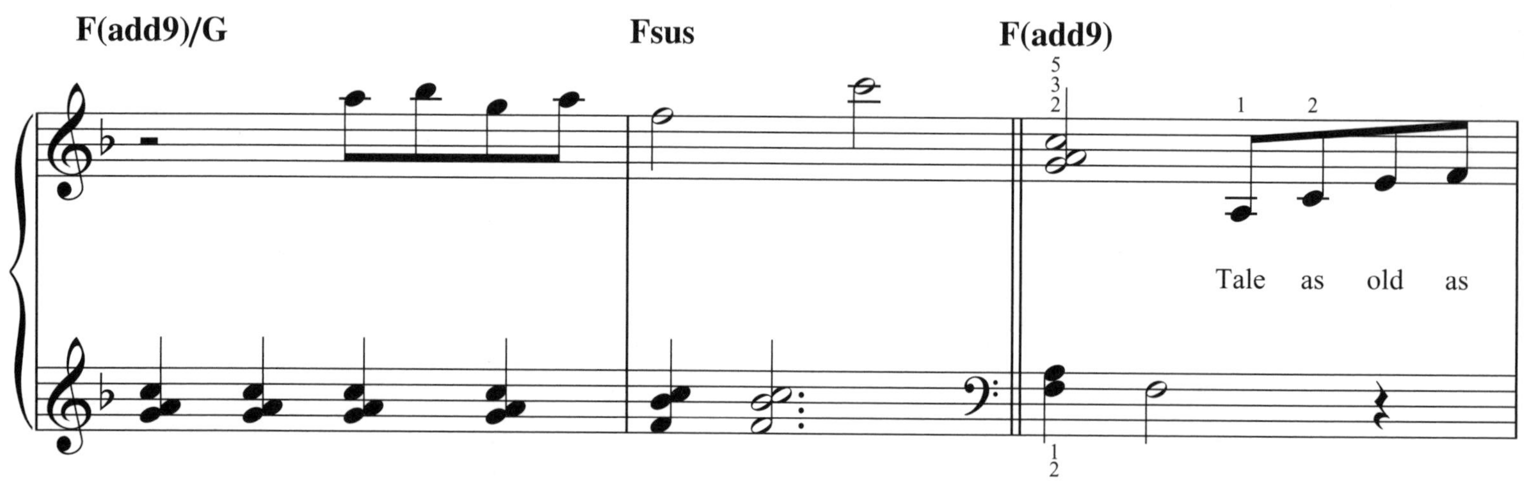

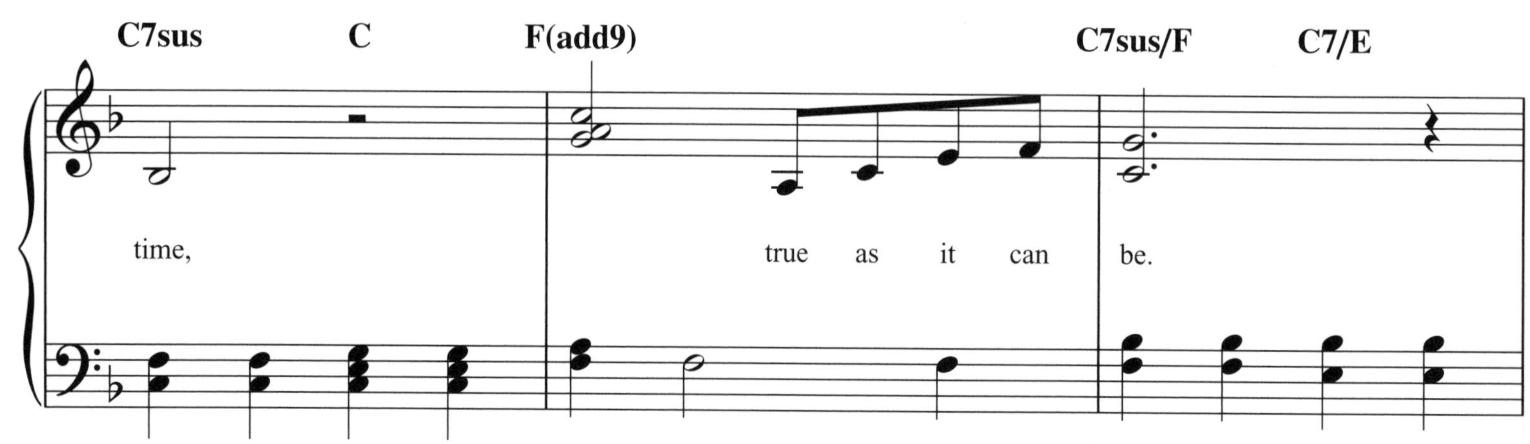

F(add9)
Am
3
3
Bare - ly e - ven friends, then some - bod - y

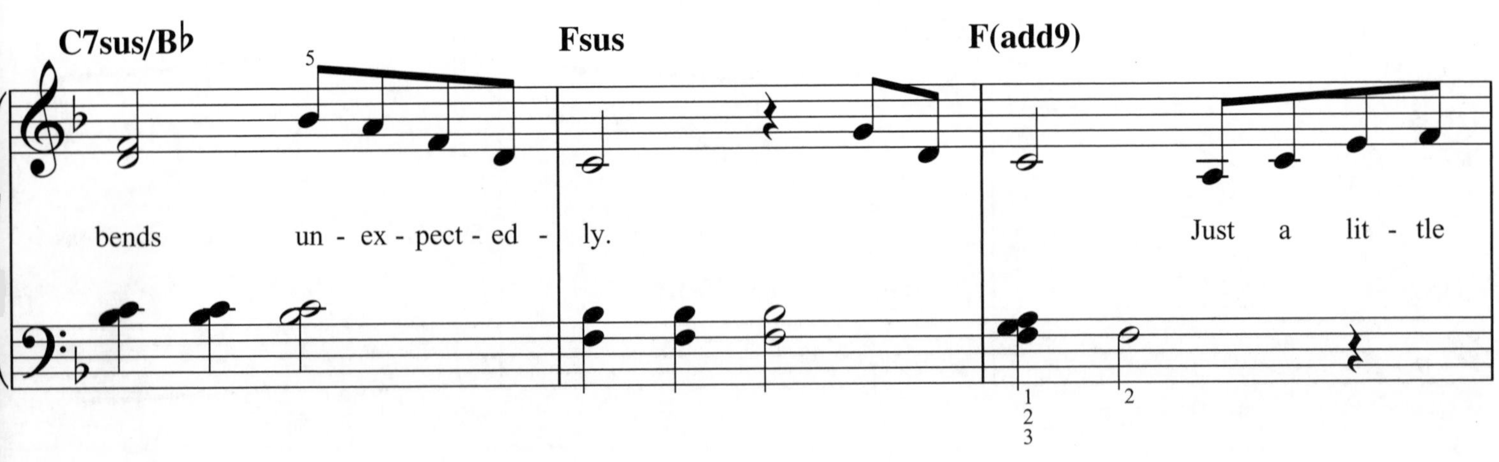
C7sus/B♭
5
Fsus
F(add9)
bends un - ex - pect - ed - ly. Just a lit - tle
1
2
3
2

C7sus
C
F(add9)
Cm7
F7/E♭
change. Small, to say the least. Both a lit - tle

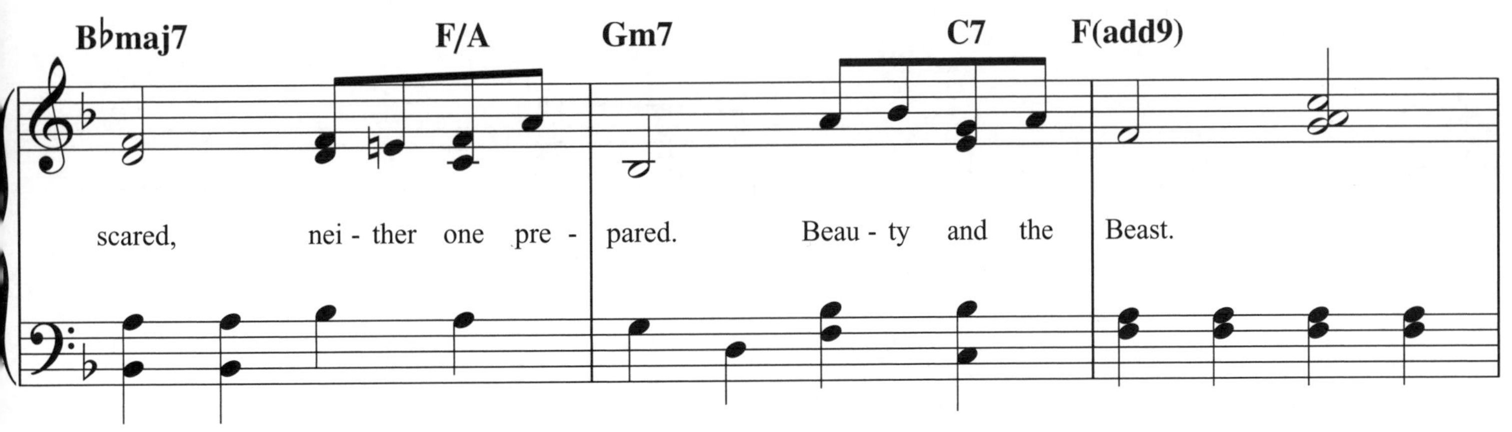
B♭maj7
F/A
Gm7
C7
F(add9)
scared, nei - ther one pre - pared. Beau - ty and the Beast.

C7sus
Am
B♭(add9)
Ev - er just the same.
Ev - er a sur -

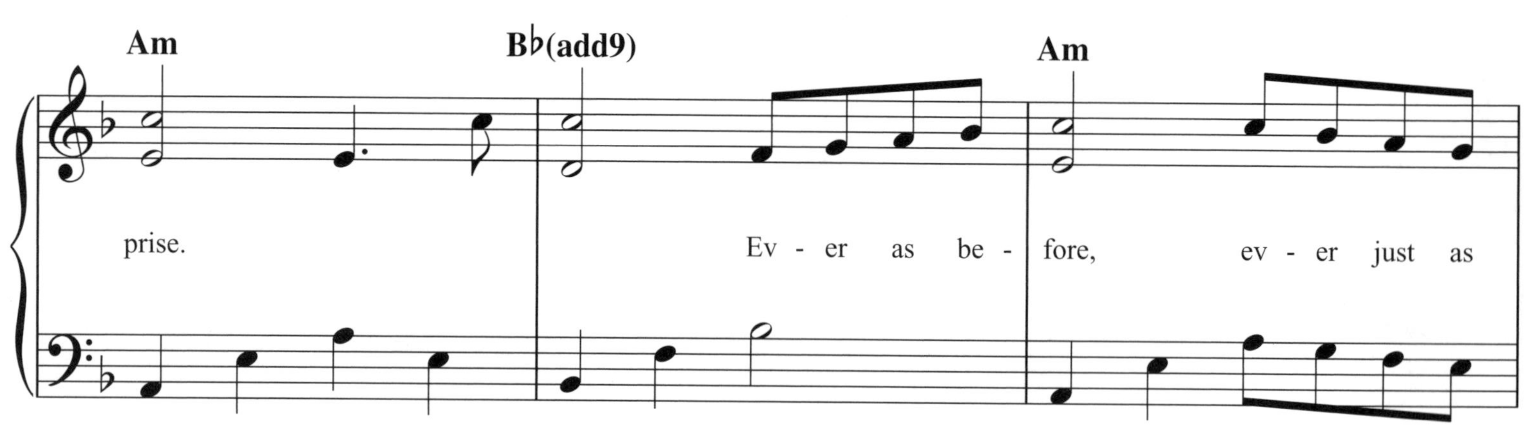
Am
B♭(add9)
Am
prise.
Ev - er as be - fore,
ev - er just as

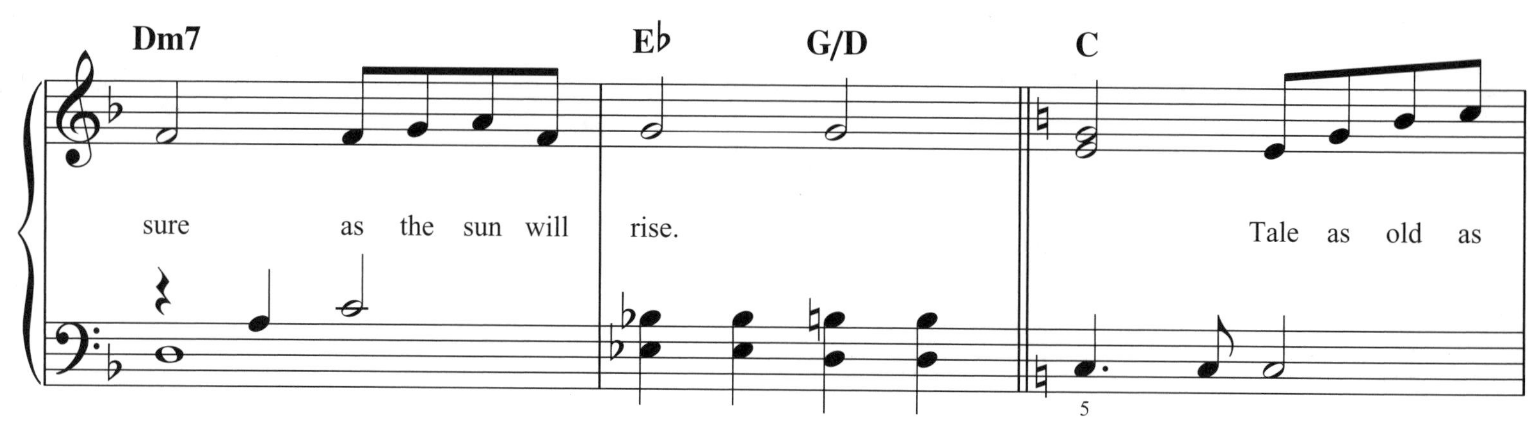
Dm7
E♭
G/D
C
sure as the sun will rise.
Tale as old as

G7sus
G
C(add9)
G7
time.
Tune as old as song.

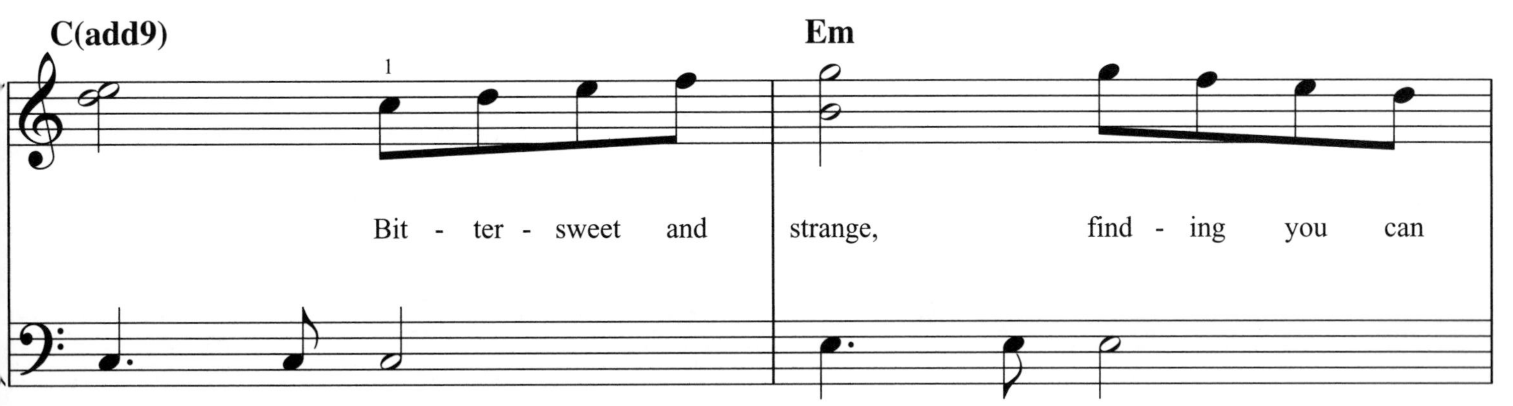
C(add9)
Em
Bit - ter - sweet and
strange, find - ing you can

F
G7/F
C
change, learn - ing you were
wrong.
Cer - tain as the

Gm7
C7
sun
ris - ing in the
East. Tale as old as

F
C/E
Dm
G7sus
G
C
time, song as old as
rhyme. Beau - ty and the
Beast.
rit.
a tempo

2.
G
F♯m7
Bm7
E7
Stand - ing here, it's oh, so clear I'm where I'm meant to

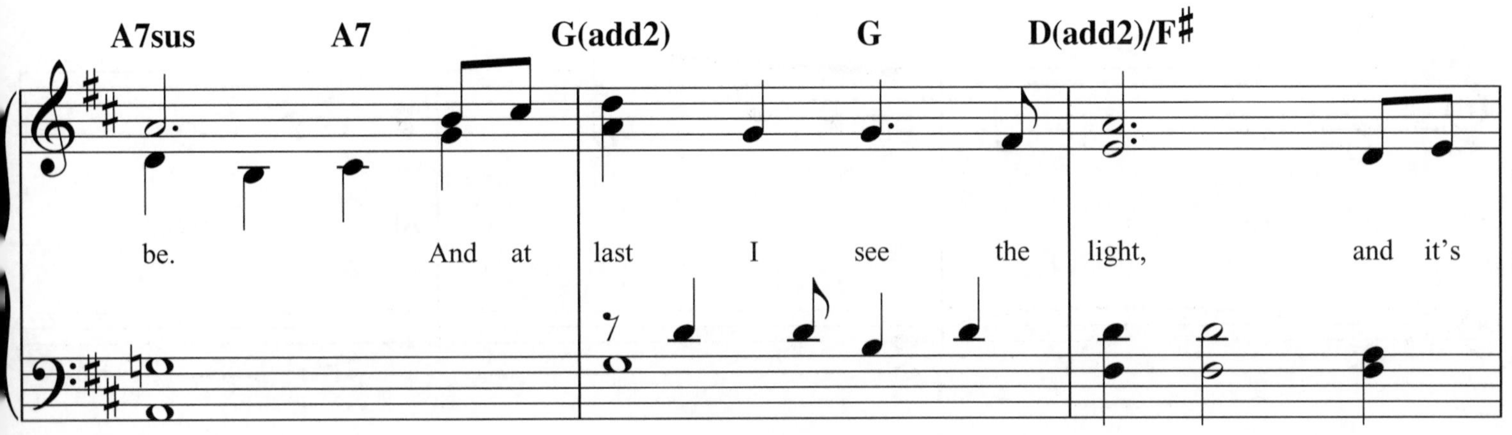
A7sus
A7
G(add2)
G
D(add2)/F♯
be. And at last I see the light, and it's

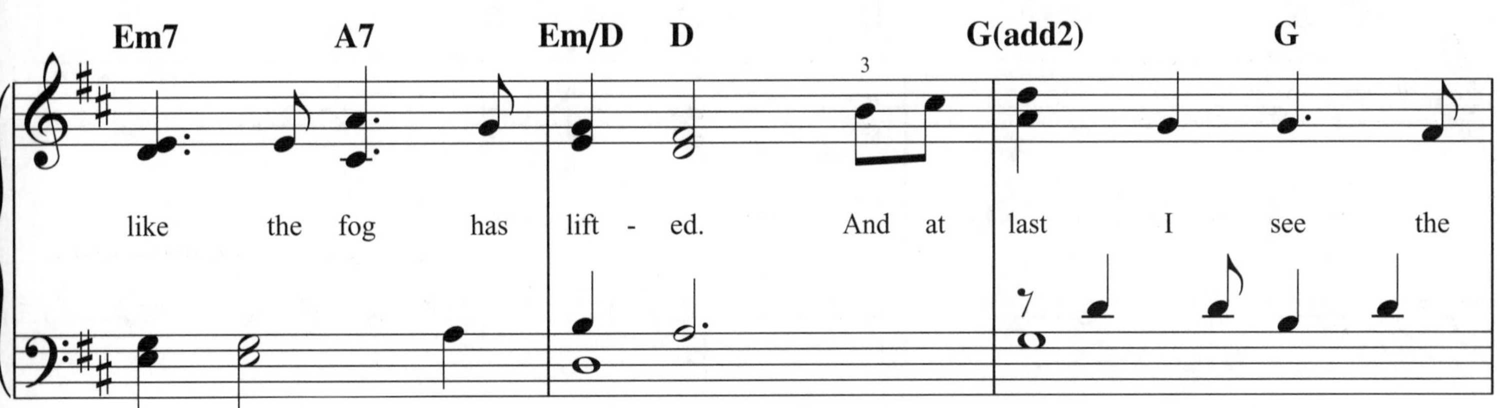
Em7
A7
Em/D
D
G(add2)
G
3
like the fog has lift - ed. And at last I see the

D(add2)
F♯sus
F♯
Bm7
light, and it's like the sky is new. And it's

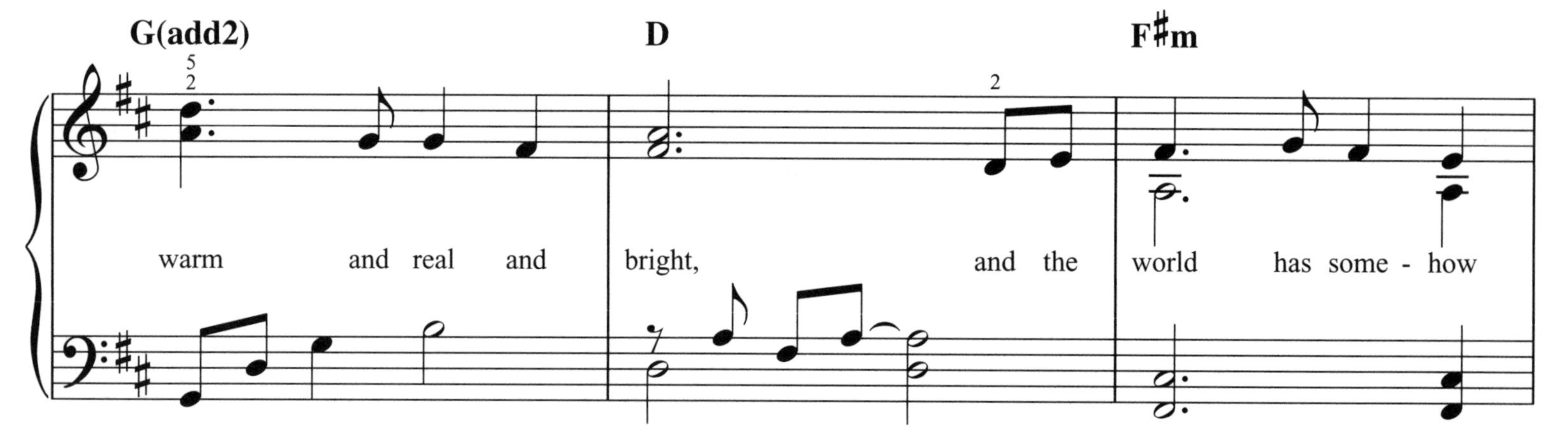
G(add2)
D
F♯m
5
2
2
warm and real and bright, and the world has some - how

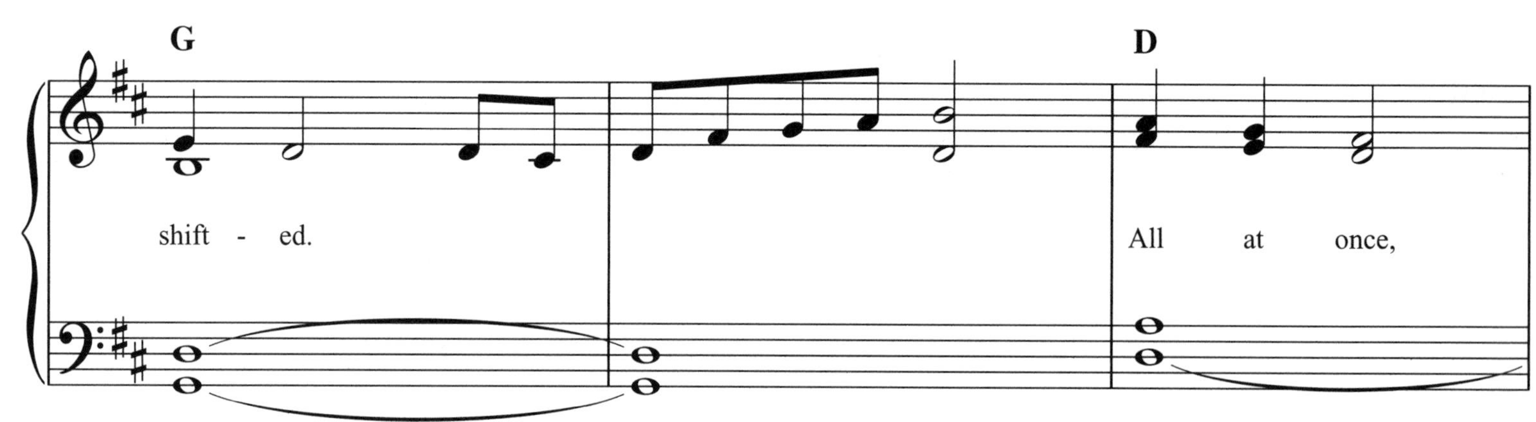
G
D
shift - ed.
All at once,

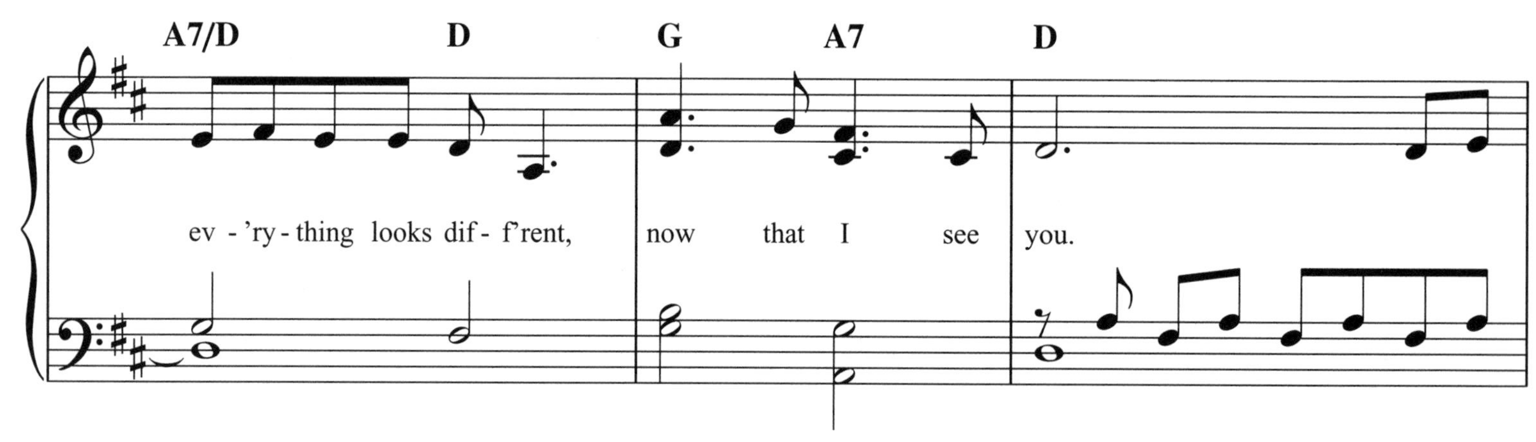
A7/D
D
G
A7
D
ev - 'ry - thing looks dif - f'rent, now that I see you.

Gm7
C7sus
F
C7/F
F
1
All those days, chas - ing down a day - dream.

F
C7/F
F
B♭
All those years
liv - ing in a blur.
All that time,

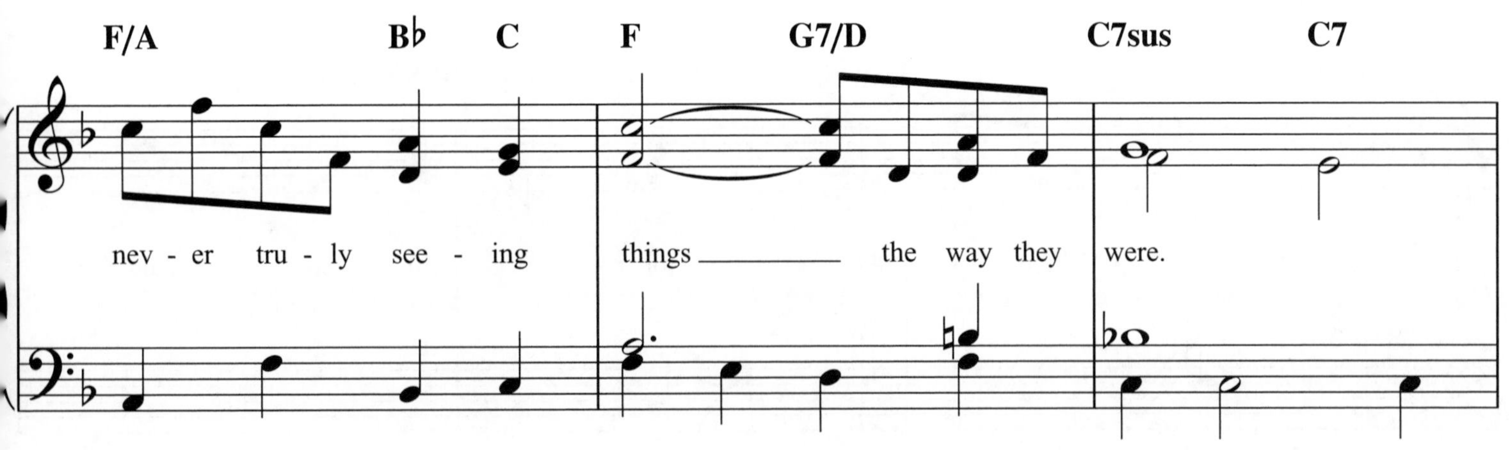
F/A
B♭
C
F
G7/D
C7sus
C7
nev - er tru - ly see - ing
things the way they
were.

F
C/F
F
Now she's here,
shin - ing in the star - light.
Now she's here;

C/F
F
B♭
Am7
F/A
sud - den - ly I know:
if she's here, it's
crys - tal clear I'm

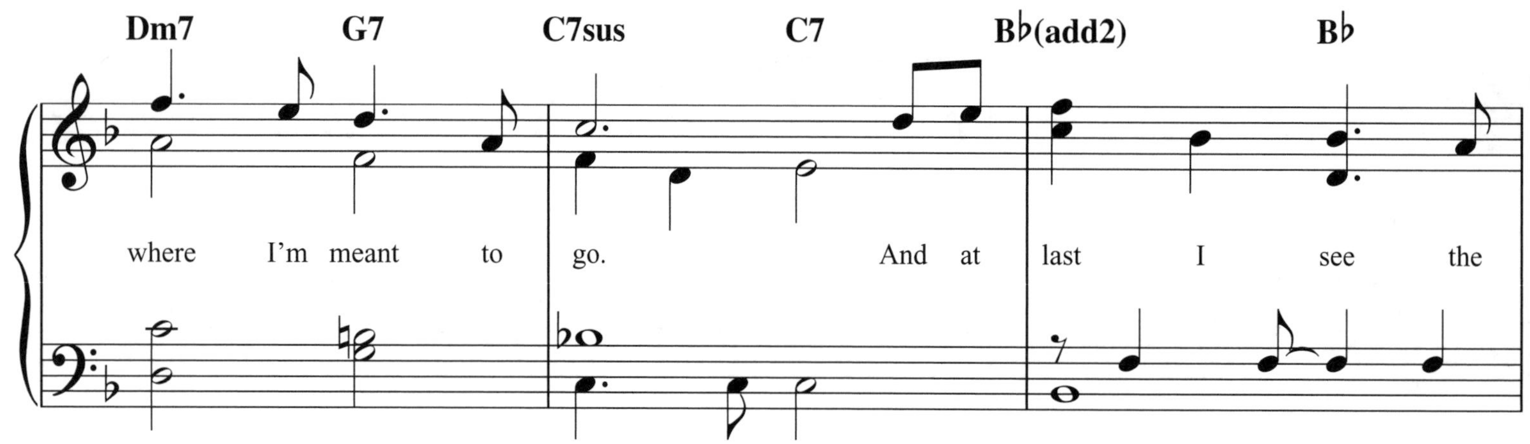
Dm7
G7
C7sus
C7
B♭(add2)
B♭
where I'm meant to go. And at last I see the

F(add2)/A
Gm7
C7sus
C7
Gm/F
F
light, and it's like the fog has lift - ed. And at

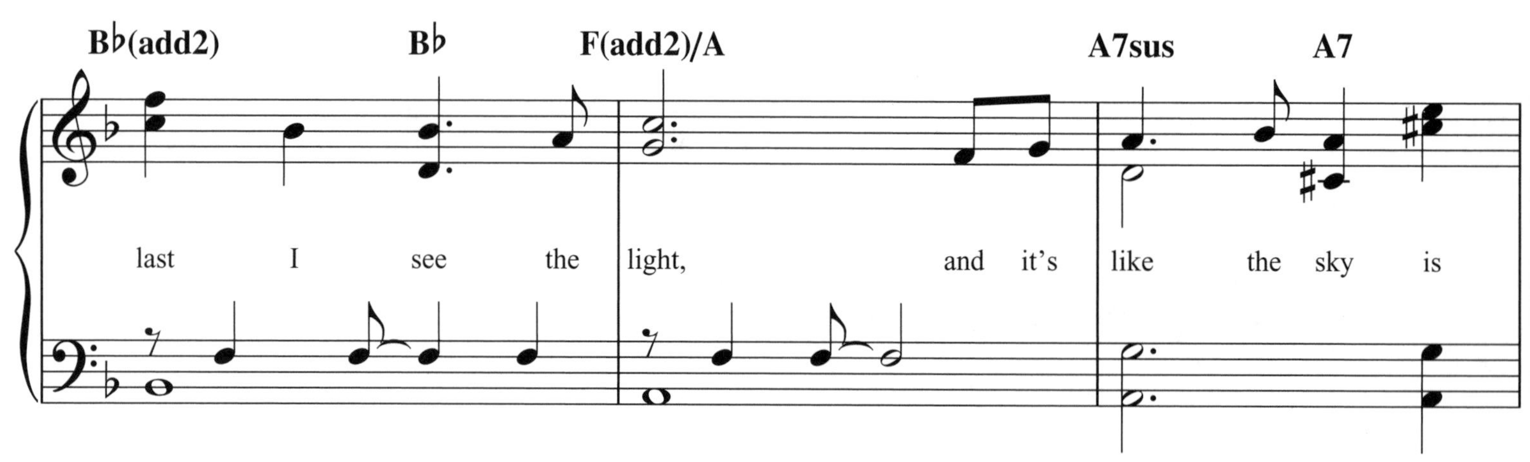
B♭(add2)
B♭
F(add2)/A
A7sus
A7
last I see the light, and it's like the sky is

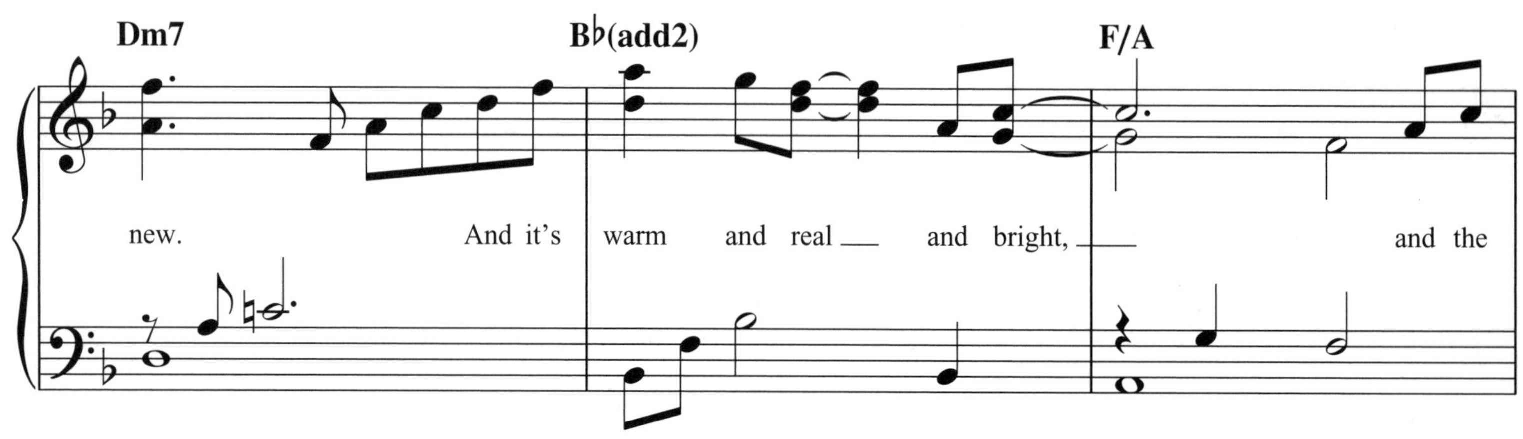
Dm7
B♭(add2)
F/A
new. And it's warm and real and bright, and the

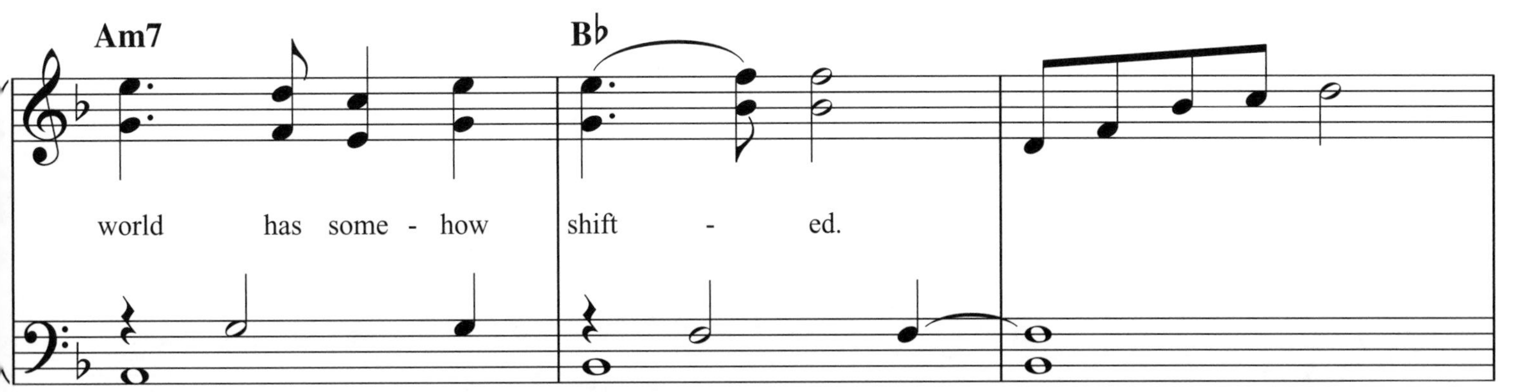
Am7
B♭
world has some - how shift - ed.

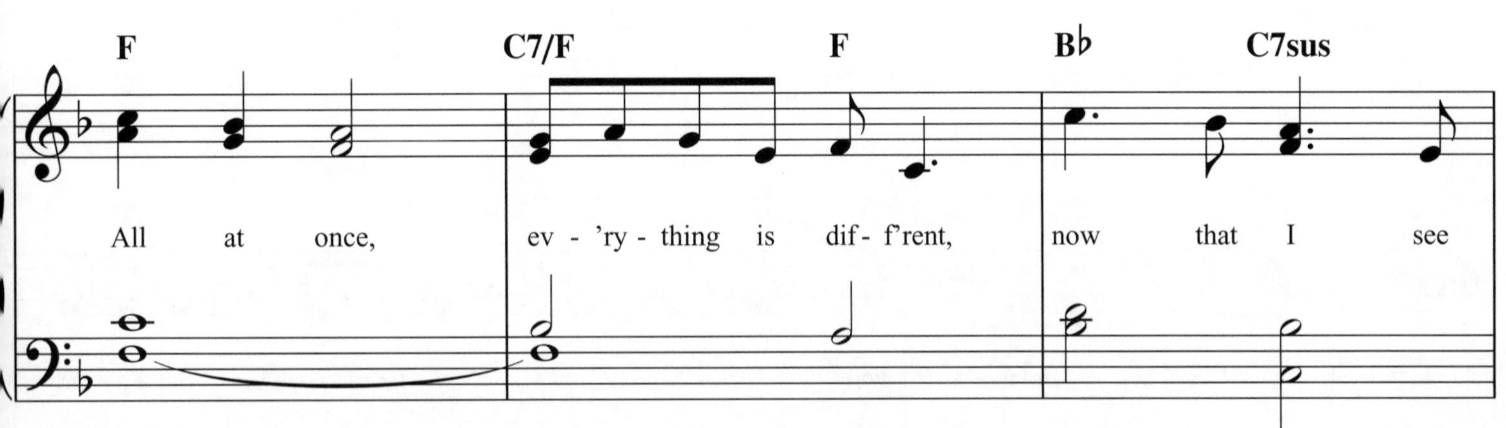
F
C7/F
F
B♭
C7sus
All at once, ev - 'ry - thing is dif - f'rent, now that I see

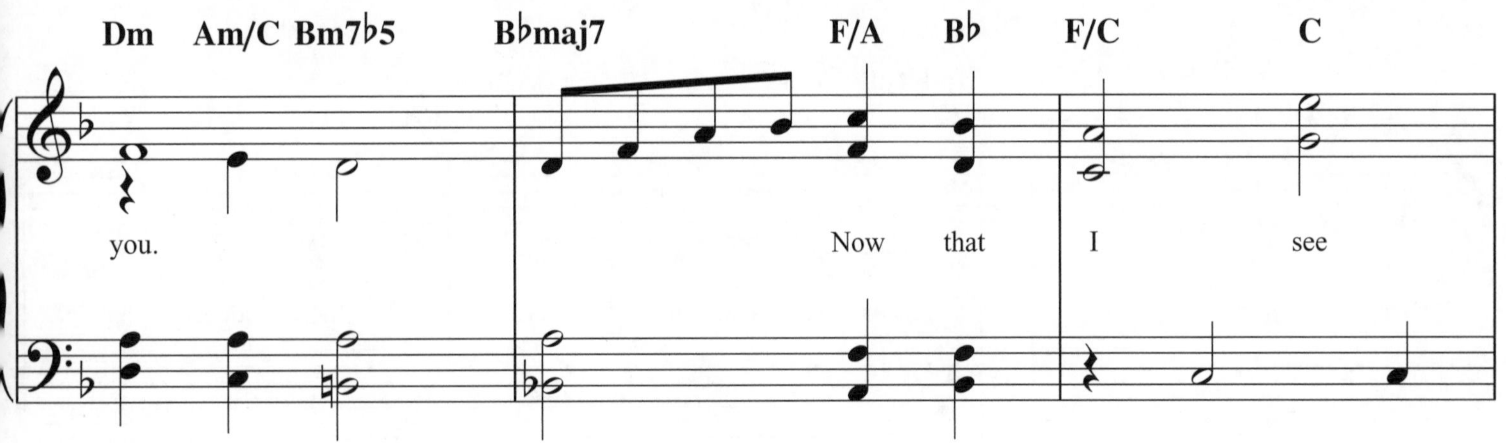
Dm
Am/C
Bm7♭5
B♭maj7
F/A
B♭
F/C
C
you. Now that I see

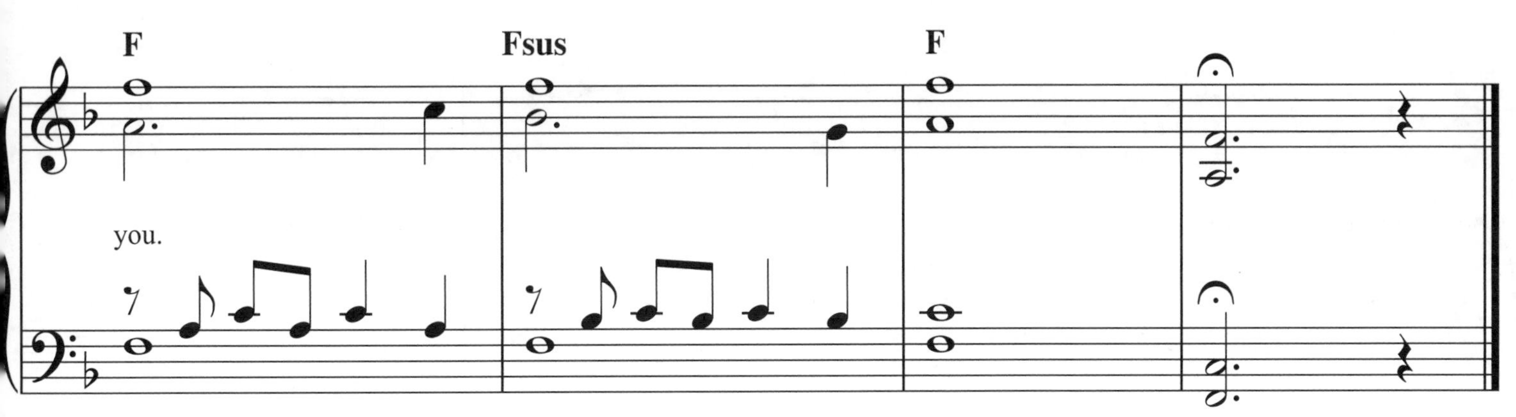
F
Fsus
F
you.

I WON'T SAY

(I'm in Love)
from HERCULES

Music by ALAN MENKEN
Lyrics by DAVID ZIPPEL

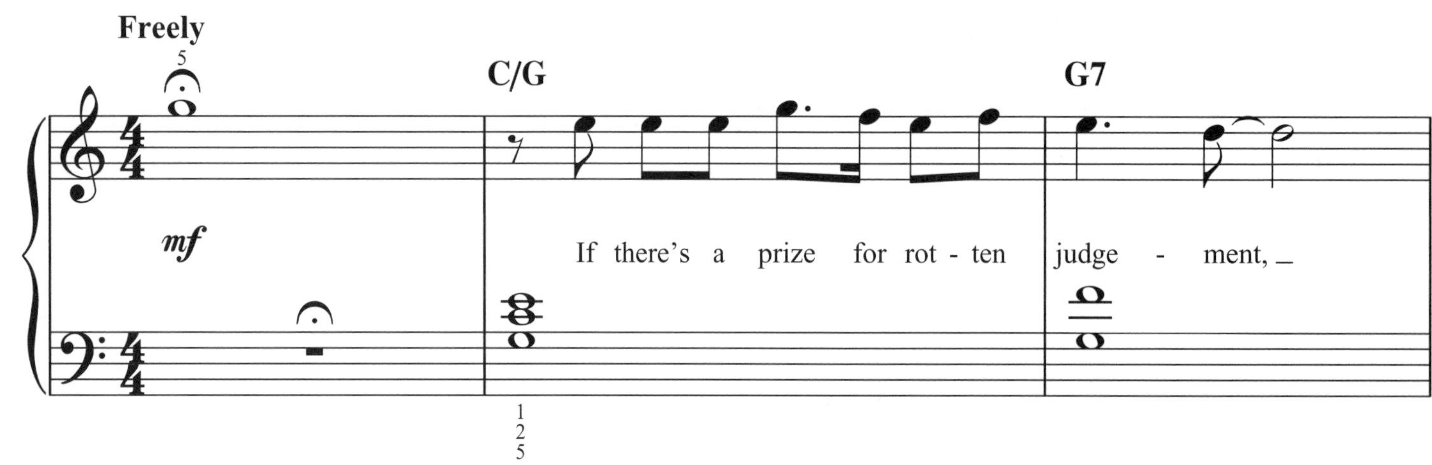

Am
Am/G
F
C/E
hon- ey, we can see right through you. Girl, ya can't con-ceal it, we know how ya feel and who you're
3

Dm7
Gsus
G
C
G/C
C
think - ing of.
No chance, no way,

G/B
Am
I won't say it, no, no. You swoon, you sigh, why de - ny it, uh

Fmaj7
G/F
Fmaj7/G
G
C
C/G G7
oh. It's too cli - ché, I won't say I'm in love.

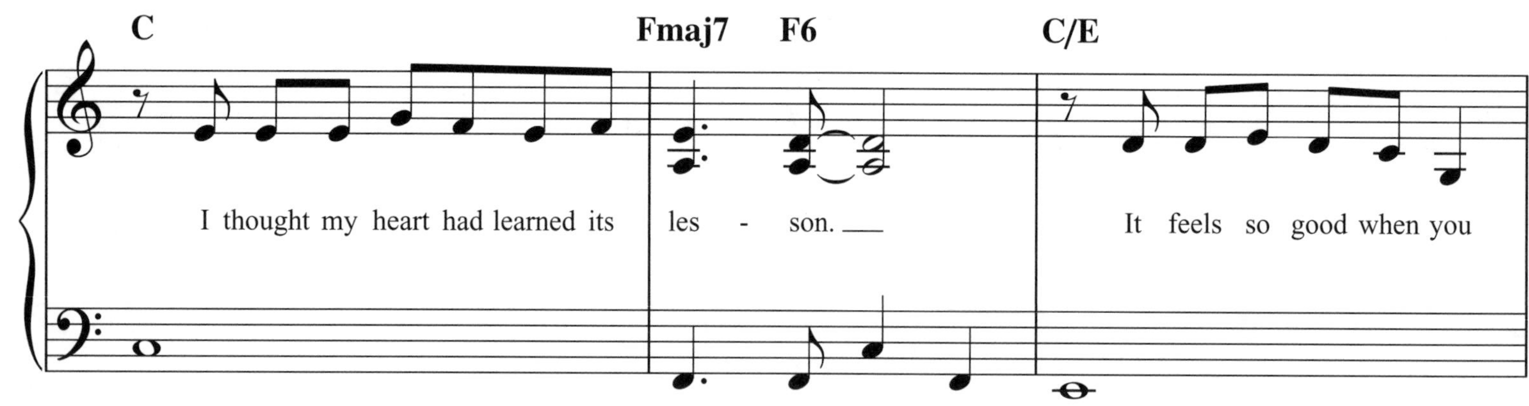
C
Fmaj7
F6
C/E
I thought my heart had learned its
les - son.
It feels so good when you

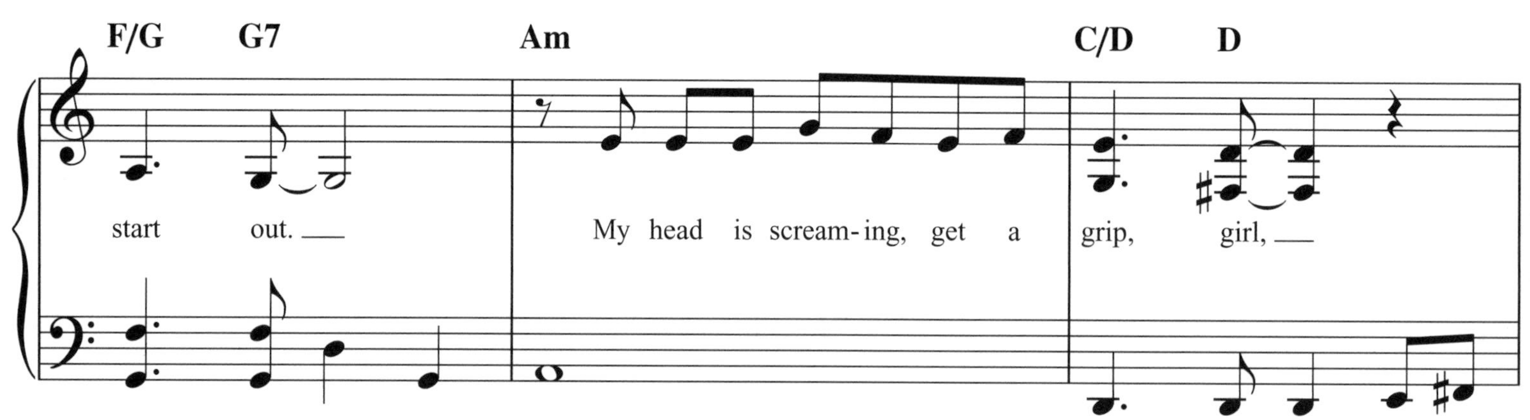
F/G
G7
Am
C/D
D
start
out.
My head is scream-ing, get a
grip,
girl,

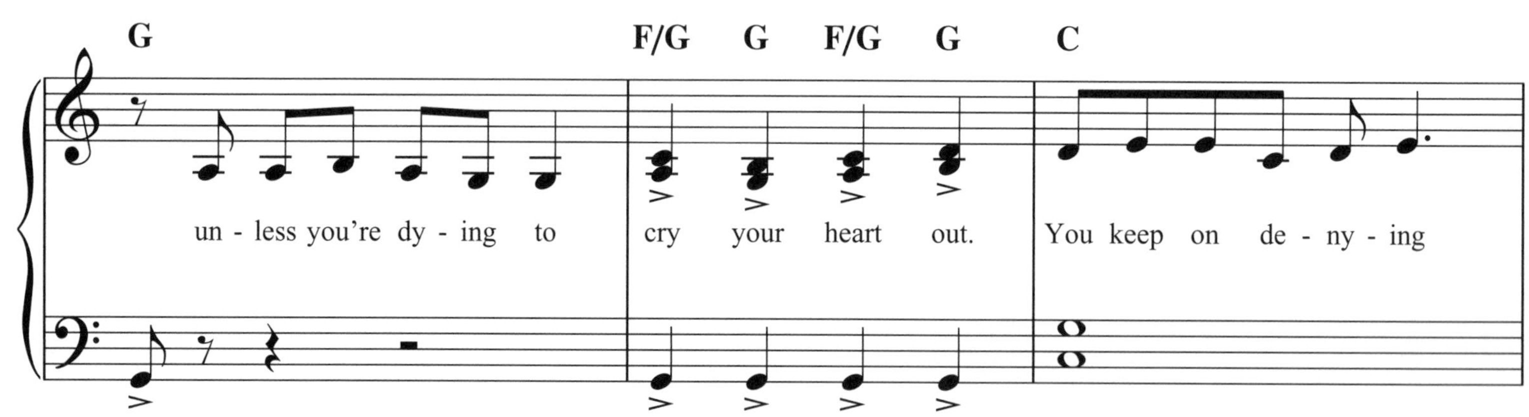
G
F/G
G
F/G
G
C
un - less you're dy - ing to
cry your heart out.
You keep on de - ny - ing

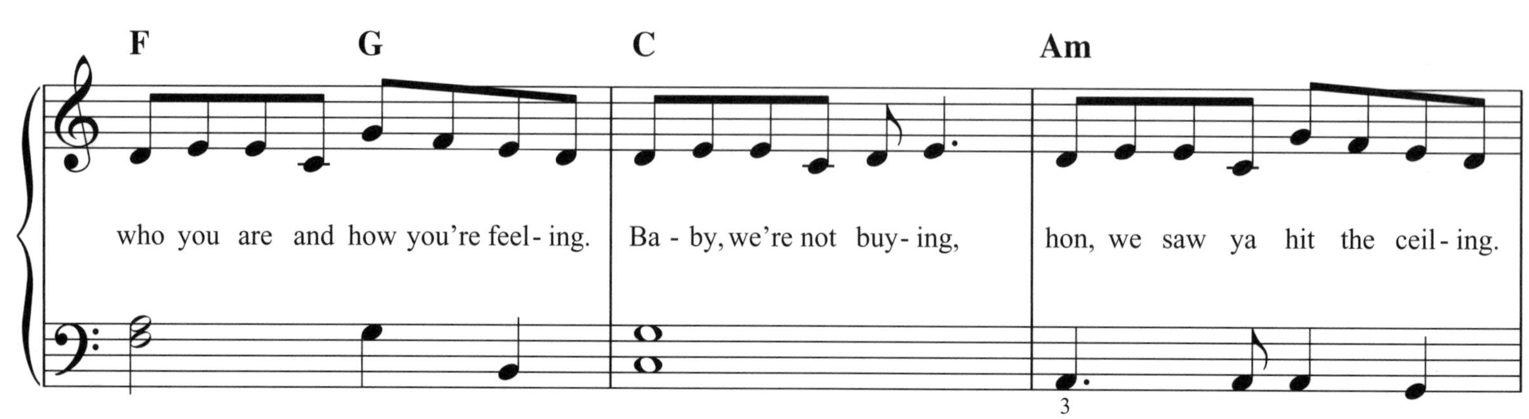
F
G
C
Am
who you are and how you're feel- ing.
Ba - by, we're not buy- ing,
hon, we saw ya hit the ceil- ing.
3

F
C/E
Dm
Face it like a grown up,
when ya gon - na own up that ya
got, got it, got it bad.

Gsus
G
C
G/C
C
G/B
No chance, no way,
I won't say it, no,

Am
Fmaj7
G/F
Fmaj7
no. Give up, give in.
Check the grin, you're in
love. This scene won't play,

F/G
G
Fmaj7/G
G
I won't say I'm in
love. You're do - in' flips,
read our lips: You're in

C
G/C
C
G/B
Am
love. You're way off base, I won't say it. Get off my case,

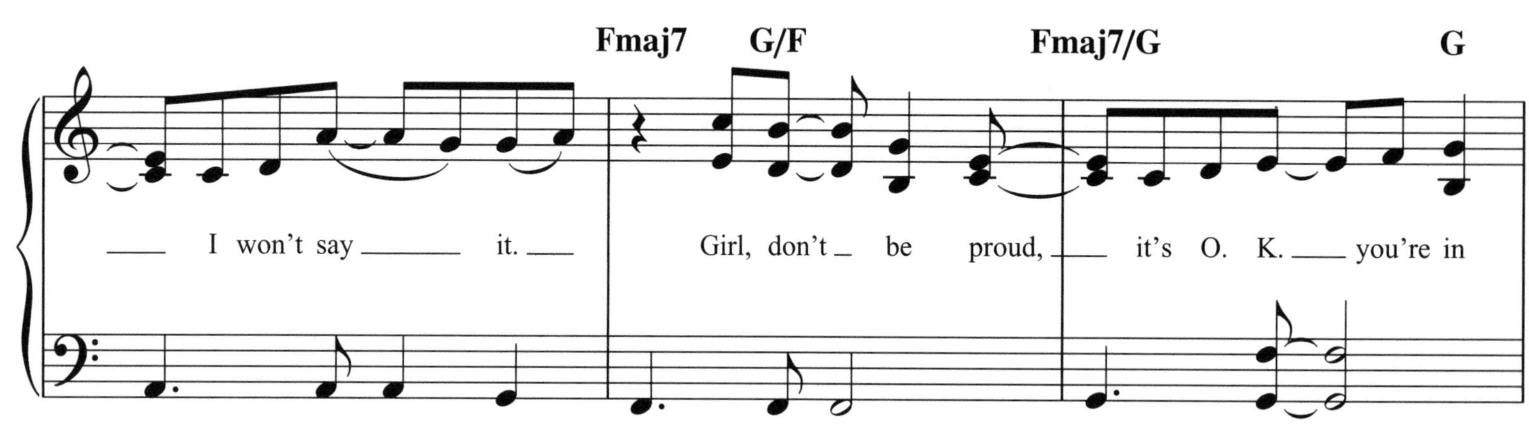
Fmaj7
G/F
Fmaj7/G
G
I won't say it. Girl, don't be proud, it's O. K. you're in

C
Am
F
G/F
Fmaj7/G
G7
love.
Oh.
rit.
At least out loud, I won't say I'm in

C
C/G
C
love.
a tempo
rit.

I'M WISHING

from SNOW WHITE AND THE SEVEN DWARFS

Words by LARRY MOREY
Music by FRANK CHURCHILL

F
hop - ing,
and I'm dream - ing

C9
of the nice things
he'll

F
Cm7
say.
Tell me, Wish - ing Well,

F7
B♭6
will my wish come true?

Dm
G7
C7
With your mag - ic spell,
won't you tell my loved one what to
do? I'm
F
wish - ing
for the one I
C9
love to
find me
to - day.
F
F(add9)
rit.

IF I NEVER KNEW YOU

from POCAHONTAS

Music by ALAN MENKEN
Lyrics by STEPHEN SCHWARTZ

G
Em
C
if I nev - er
felt this love, __
I would have no

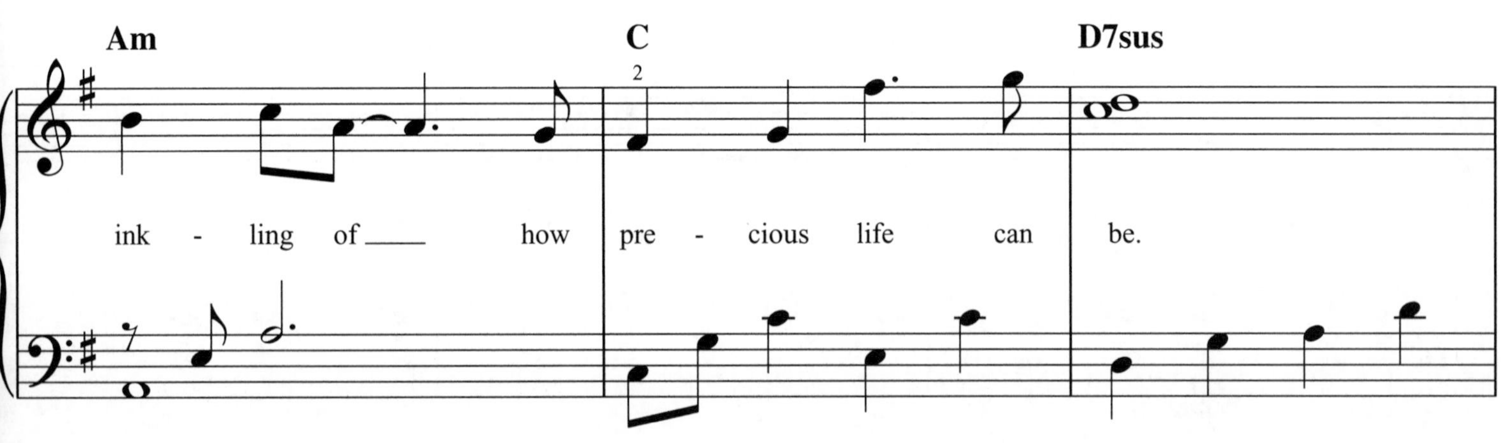
Am
C
D7sus
ink - ling of ___ how
pre - cious life can
be.

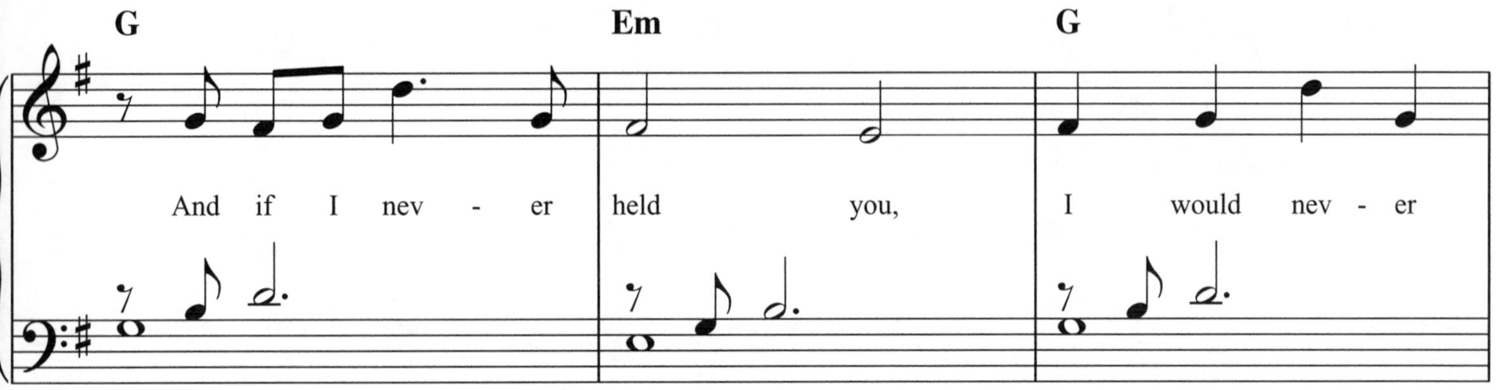
G
Em
G
And if I nev - er
held you,
I would nev - er

Em
E/G♯
Am
Cm(maj7)
Cm6
have a clue ___
how, at last ___ I'd
find in you

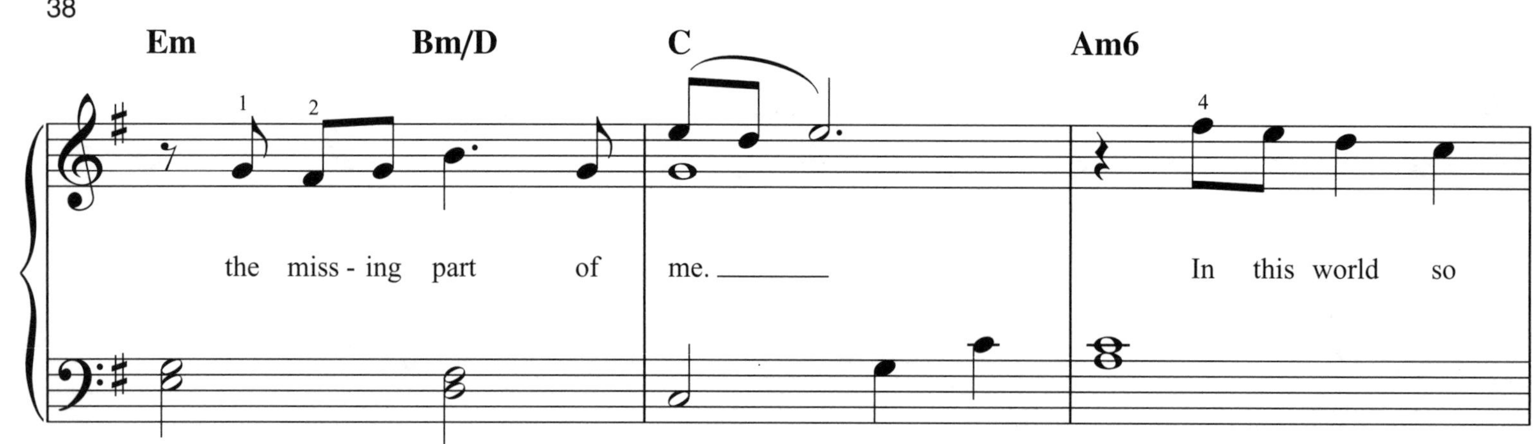
Em Bm/D C Am6
the miss - ing part of me. In this world so

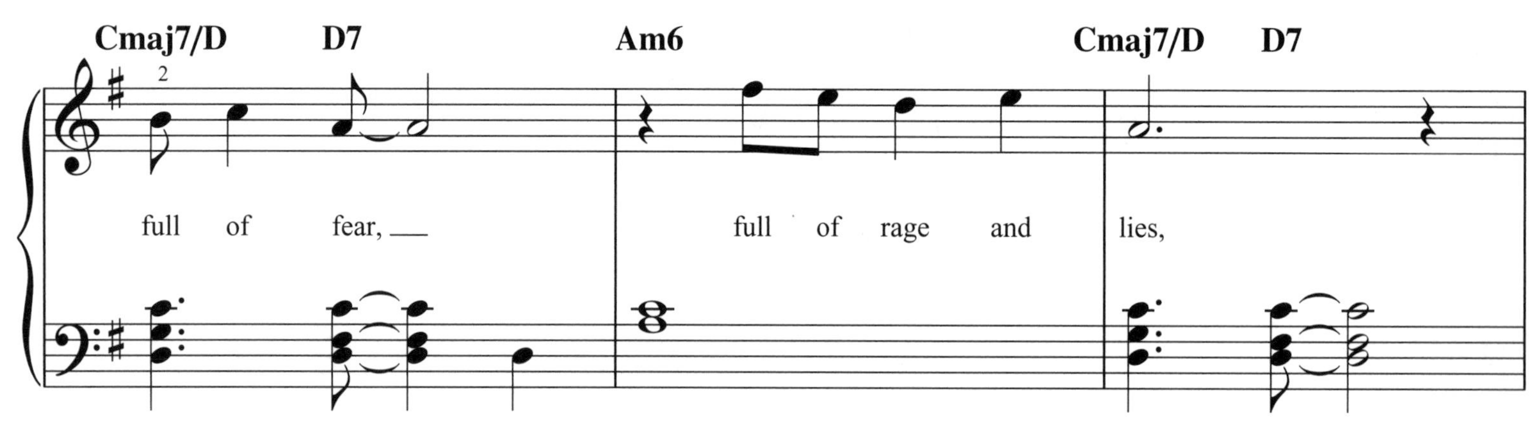
Cmaj7/D D7 Am6 Cmaj7/D D7
full of fear, full of rage and lies,

Bm7/F♯ B7/D♯ Em Em7 C
I can see the truth so clear in your eyes, so

D C/D G Em
dry your eyes. And I'm so grate - ful to you.

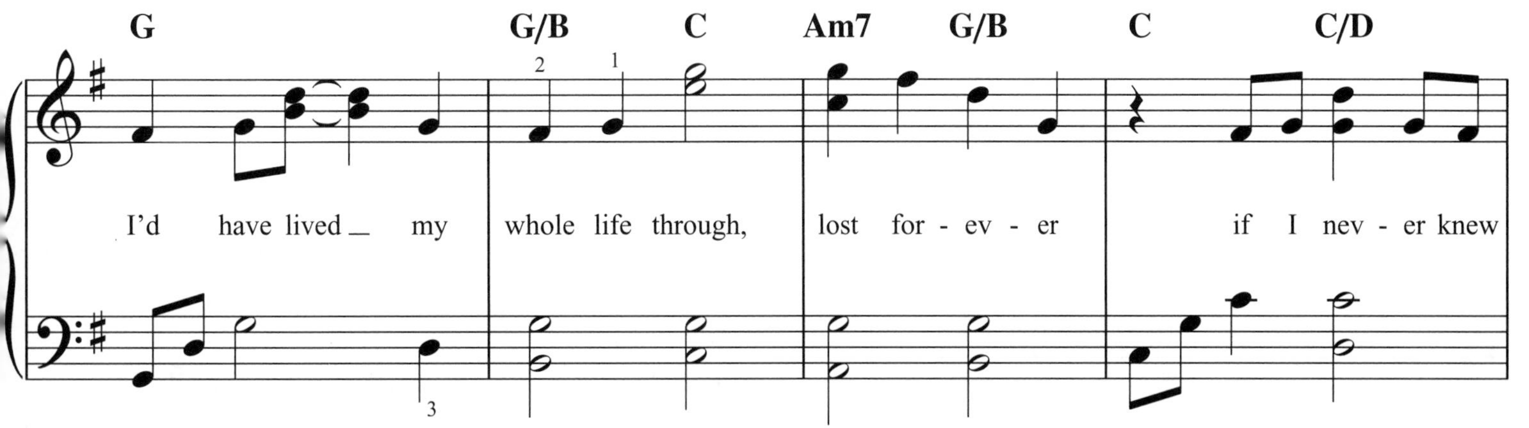
G
G/B
C
Am7
G/B
C
C/D
I'd have lived __ my whole life through, lost for - ev - er if I nev - er knew

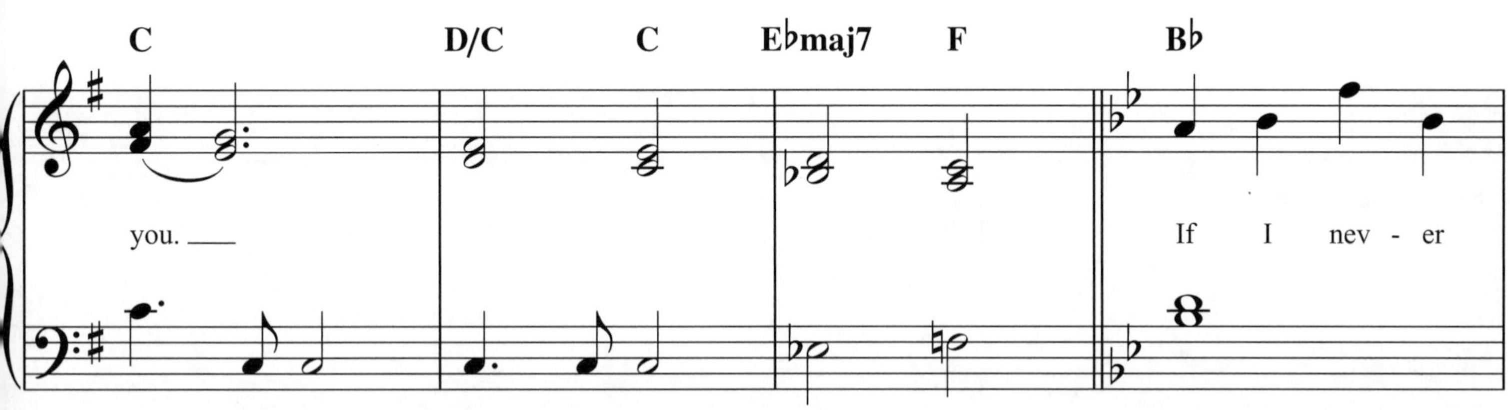
C
D/C
C
E♭maj7
F
B♭
you. __
If I nev - er

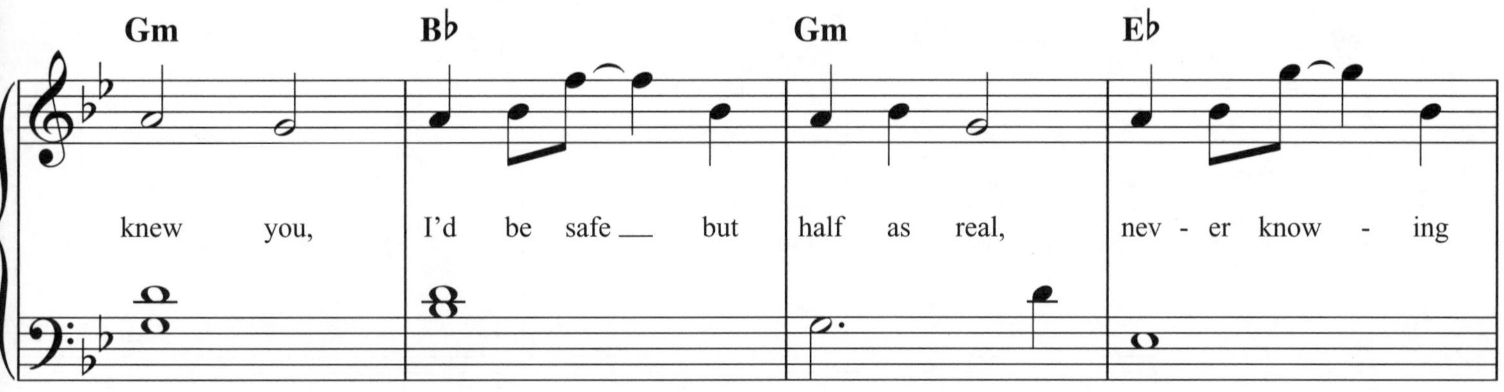
Gm
B♭
Gm
E♭
knew you, I'd be safe __ but half as real, nev - er know - ing

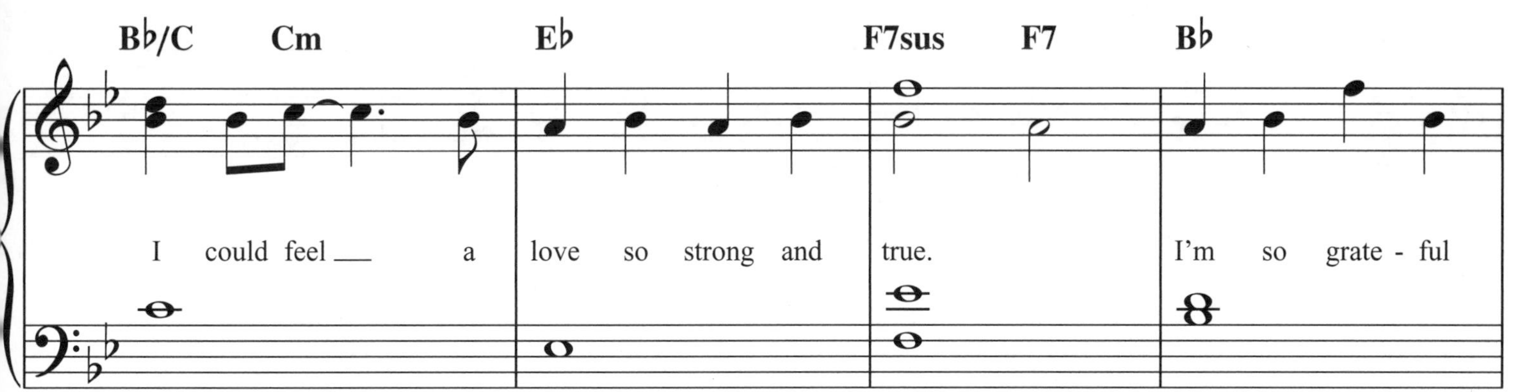
B♭/C
Cm
E♭
F7sus
F7
B♭
I could feel __ a love so strong and true. I'm so grate - ful

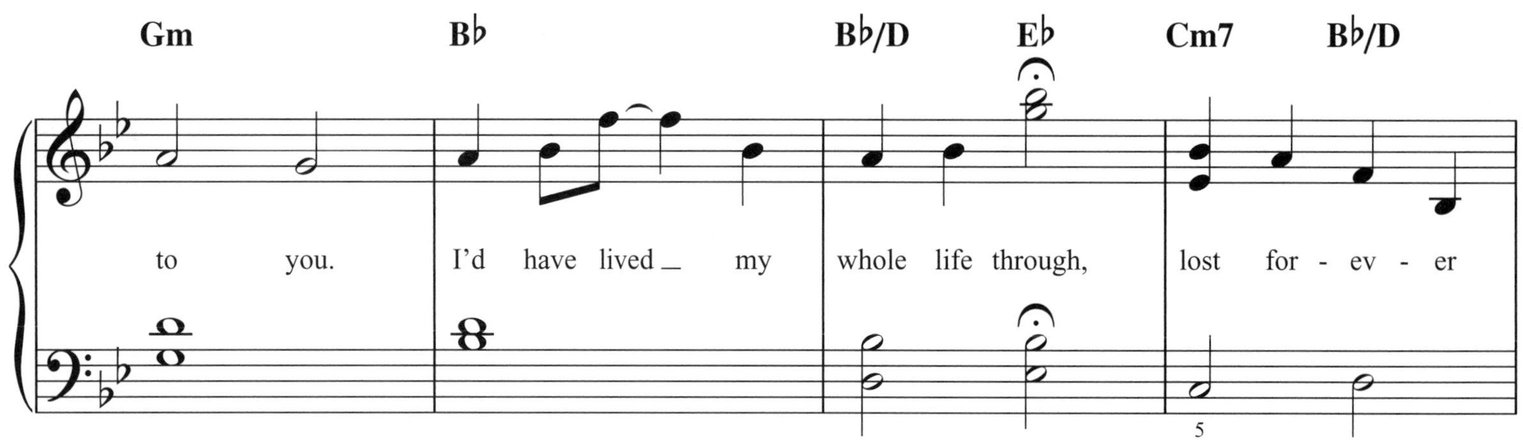
Gm
B♭
B♭/D
E♭
Cm7
B♭/D
to you. I'd have lived _ my whole life through, lost for - ev - er
5

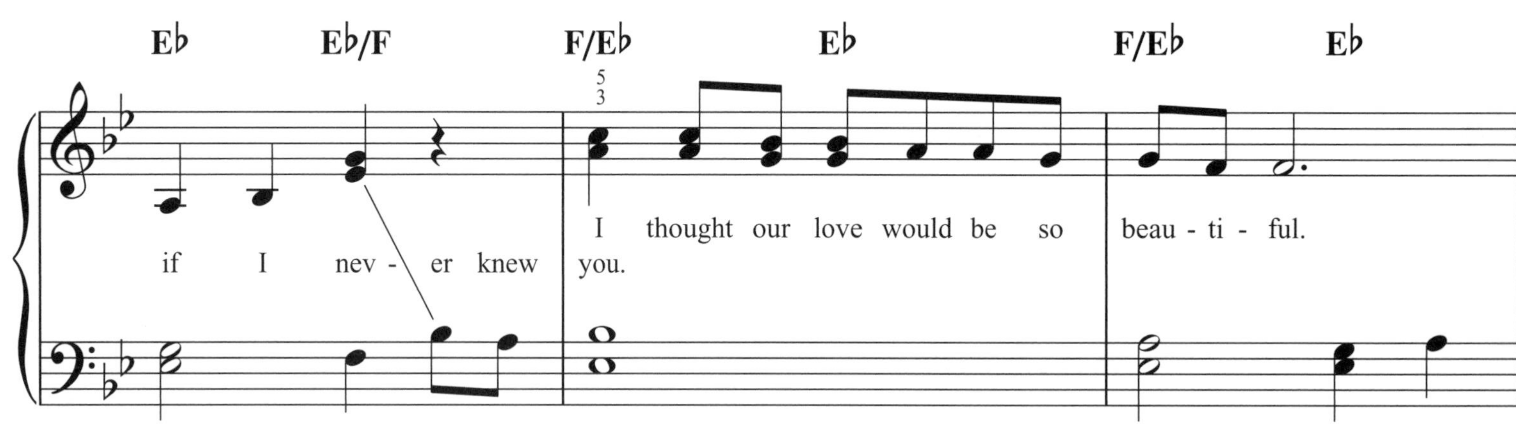
E♭
E♭/F
F/E♭
E♭
F/E♭
E♭
5
3
if I nev - er knew you.
I thought our love would be so beau - ti - ful.

Dm7
Gm
3
Some - how we'd make the whole world bright. _ I nev - er knew that fear and

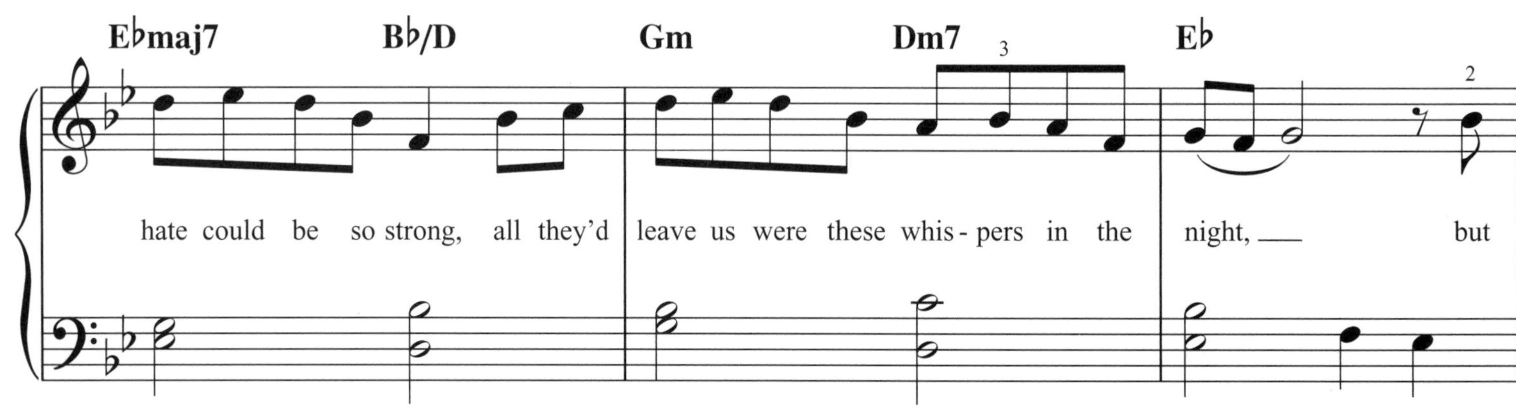
E♭maj7
B♭/D
Gm
Dm7
E♭
3
2
hate could be so strong, all they'd leave us were these whis - pers in the night, _ but

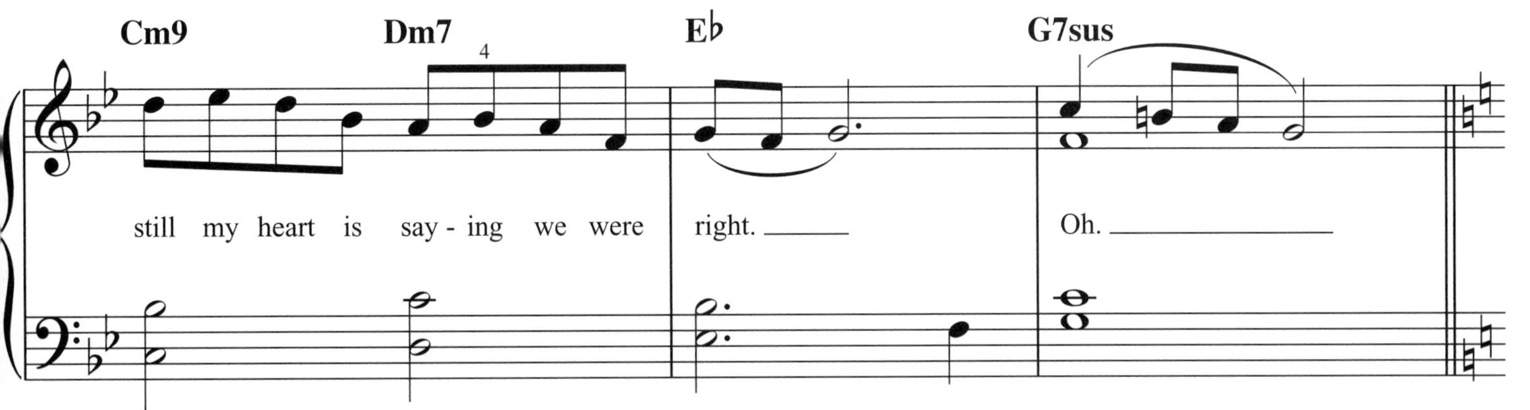
Cm9
Dm7
E♭
G7sus
4
still my heart is say - ing we were right. ___ Oh. ___

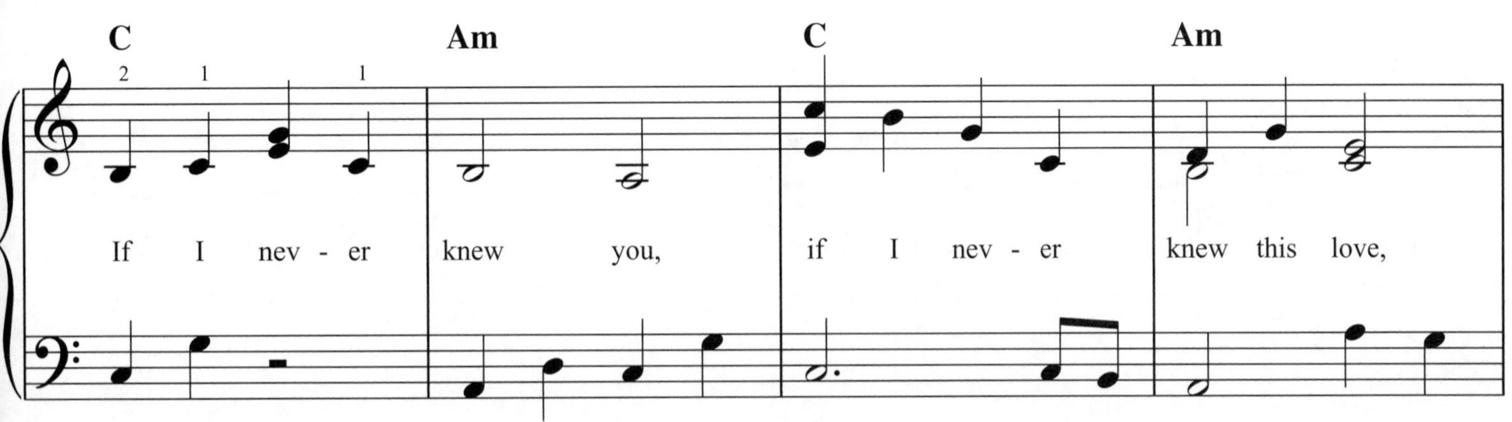
C
Am
C
Am
2 1 1
If I nev - er knew you, if I nev - er knew this love,

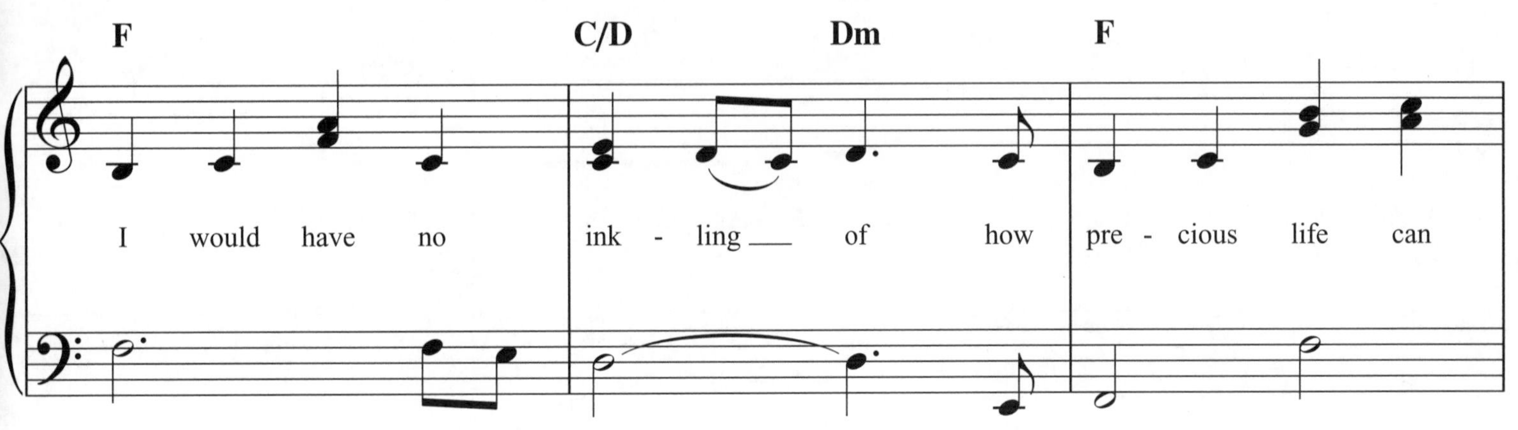
F
C/D
Dm
F
I would have no ink - ling ___ of how pre - cious life can

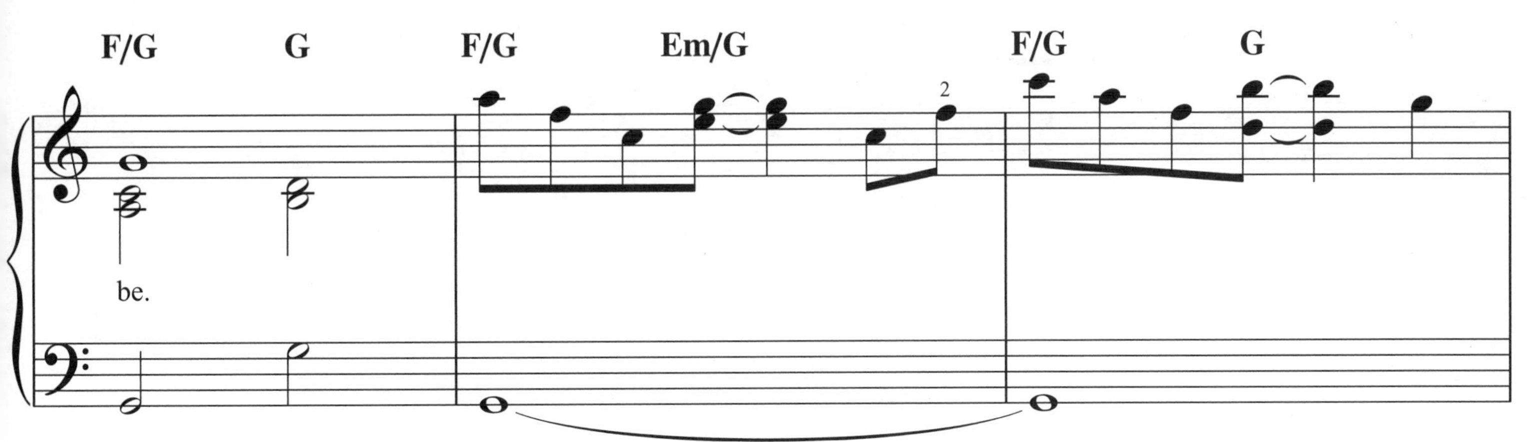
F/G
G
F/G
Em/G
F/G
G
2
be.

F/G
G
G/F
F
I thought our love would be so beau - ti - ful,

Em7
G/F
F
some - how we'd make the whole world bright.
I thought our love would be so

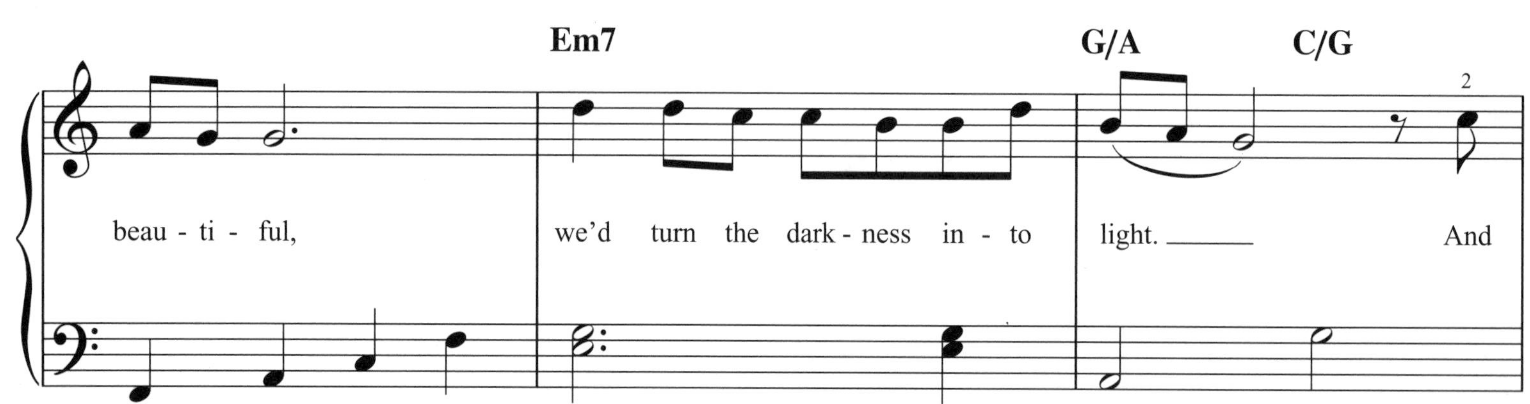
Em7
G/A
C/G
beau - ti - ful,
we'd turn the dark - ness in - to light.
And

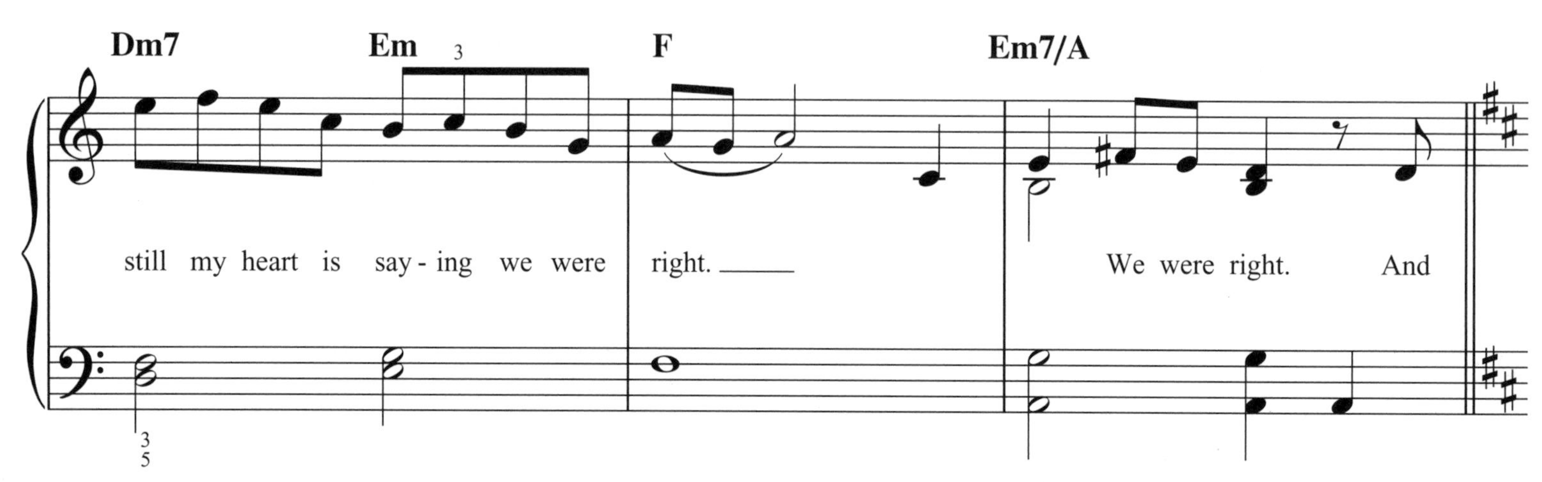
Dm7
Em
F
Em7/A
still my heart is say - ing we were right.
We were right. And

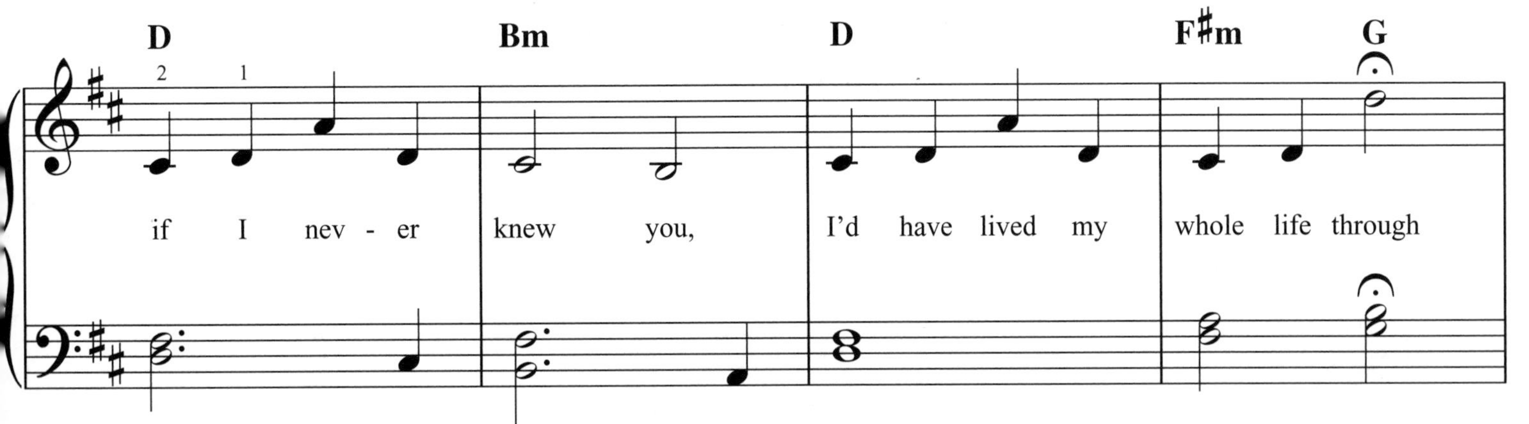
D
Bm
D
F♯m
G
2 1
if I nev - er knew you, I'd have lived my whole life through

Em7
F♯m7
G
Em7
F♯m7
emp - ty as ___ the sky, nev - er know - ing

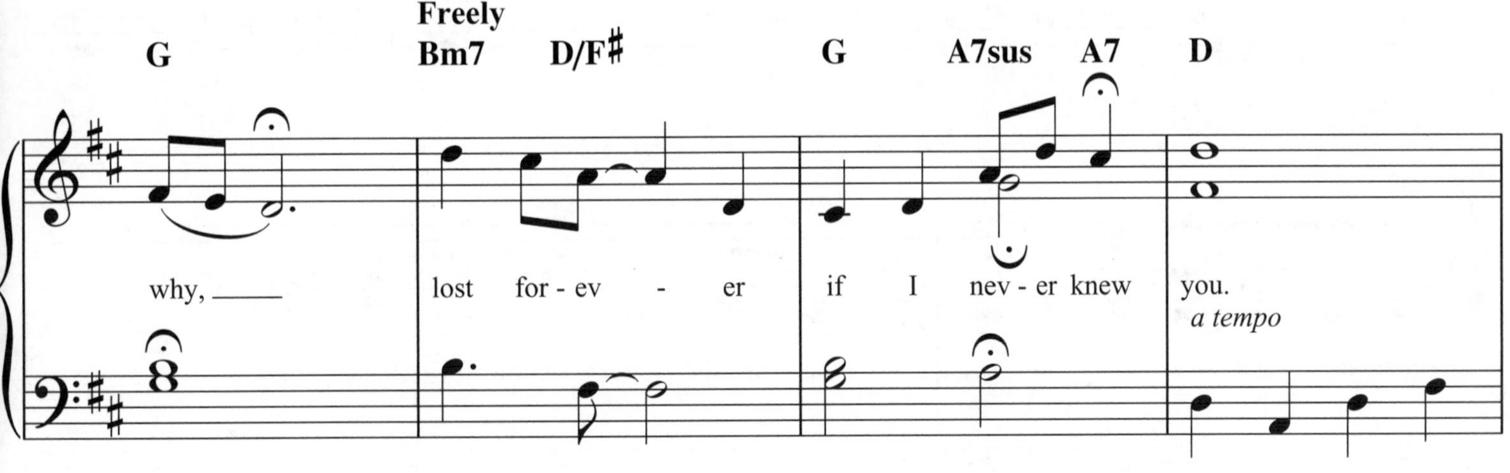
Freely
G
Bm7
D/F♯
G
A7sus
A7
D
why, ___ lost for - ev - er if I nev - er knew you.
a tempo

Bm
G
A7sus
A7
D
1
rit.

KISS THE GIRL
from THE LITTLE MERMAID

Music by ALAN MENKEN
Lyrics by HOWARD ASHMAN

2
Yes, you want her. Look at her, you know you

Gm
F
do. Pos - si - ble she wants you, too. There is one way to

C
G7
3
ask her. It don't take a word, not a sin - gle word, go on and

C
2
1
kiss the girl. Sha la la la la la,

F
C
G7
my oh my, look like the boy too shy. Ain't gon - na kiss the girl.

C
F
G7
Sha la la la la la, ain't that sad. Ain't it a shame, too bad. He gon - na

C
miss the girl.

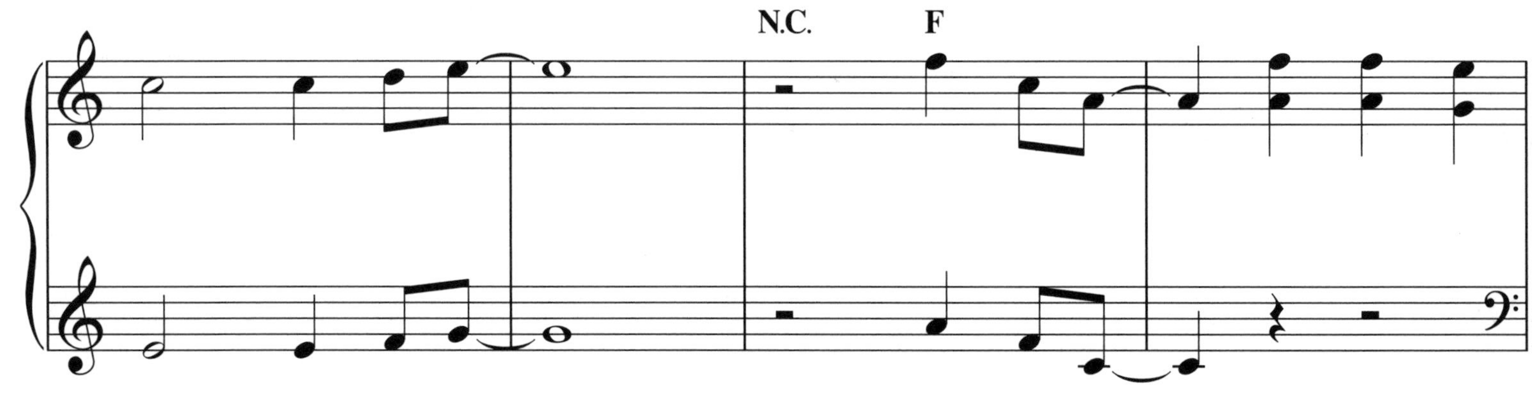
N.C.
F

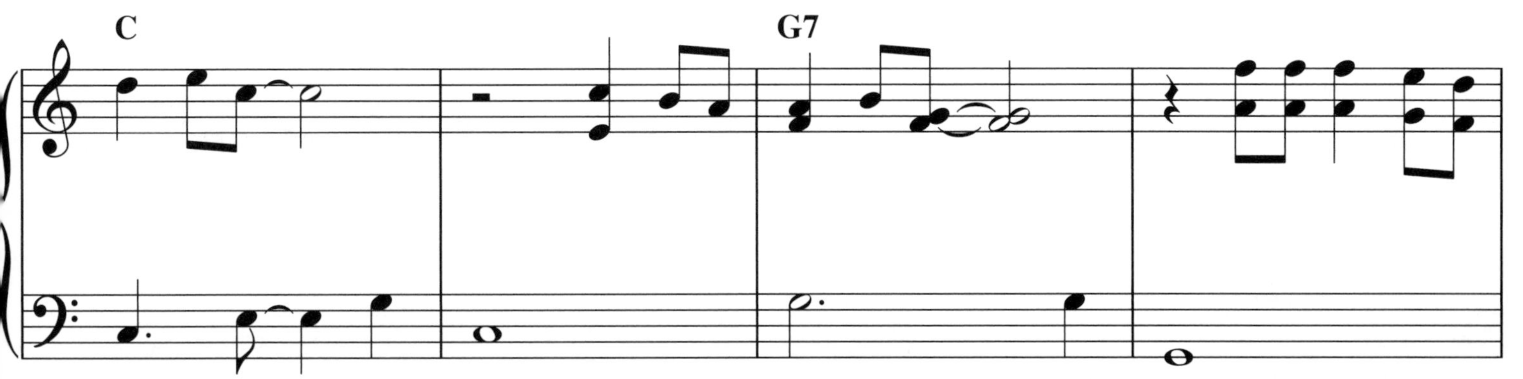
C
G7

C
4
2

G
C
G
Now's your mo - ment, float - ing in a blue la -

C
Gm
F
goon. Boy, you bet - ter do it soon, no time will be

C
G7
3
bet - ter.
She don't
say a word and she
2

C
4
1
3
won't say a word un - til you
kiss the girl.

C
F
C
2
1
Sha la la la la la,
Sha la la la la la,
don't be scared. You got the
float a - long. And lis - ten
mood pre - pared, go on and
to the song, the song say
2
1

G7
C
F
4
kiss the girl.
kiss the girl.
Sha la la la la la,
Sha la la la la the
don't stop now. Don't try to
mu - sic play. Do what the

1.
2.
G7
C
C
hide it how you wan - na
mu - sic say. You got - ta
kiss the girl.
kiss the girl.
1

You've got to
kiss the girl.
You wan - na
2

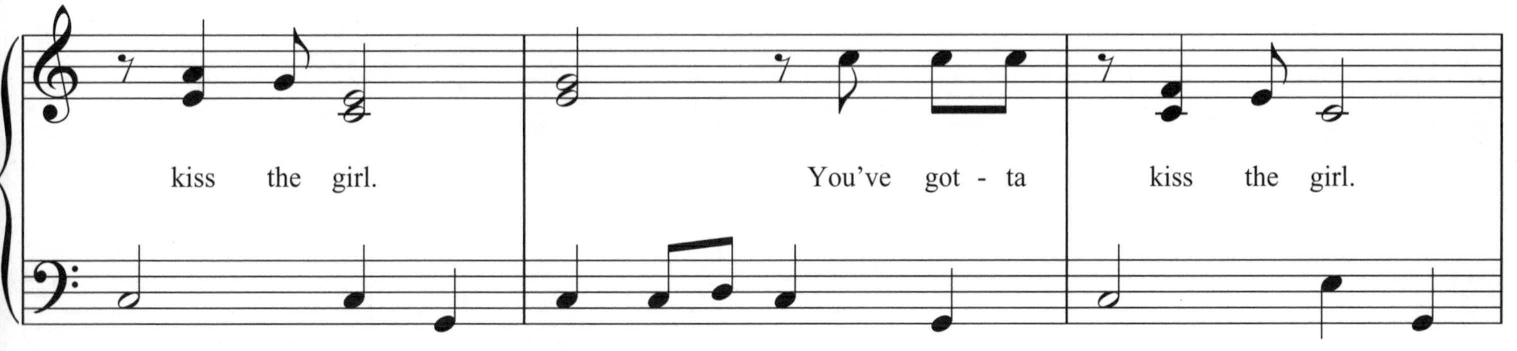
kiss the girl.
You've got - ta
kiss the girl.

G7
C
3
1
Go on and
kiss the girl.

LOVE
from ROBIN HOOD

Words by FLOYD HUDDLESTON
Music by GEORGE BRUNS

Moderately, in 2

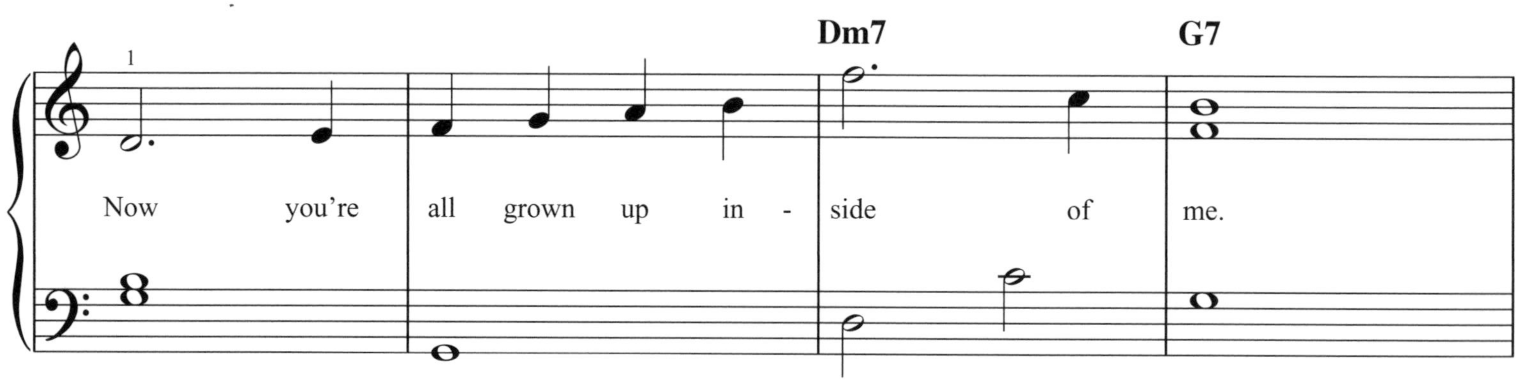

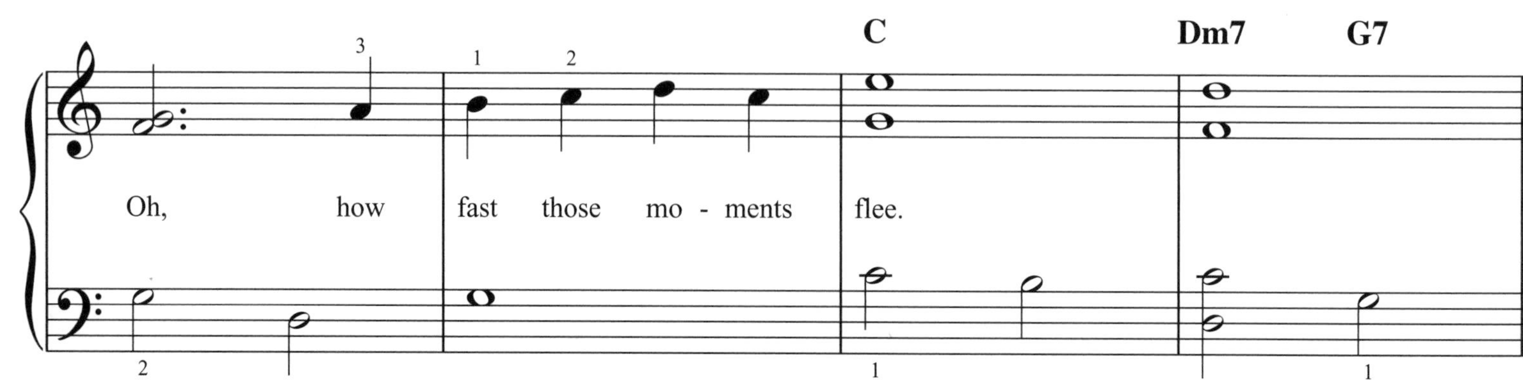

C
Once we watched a la - zy world go by.

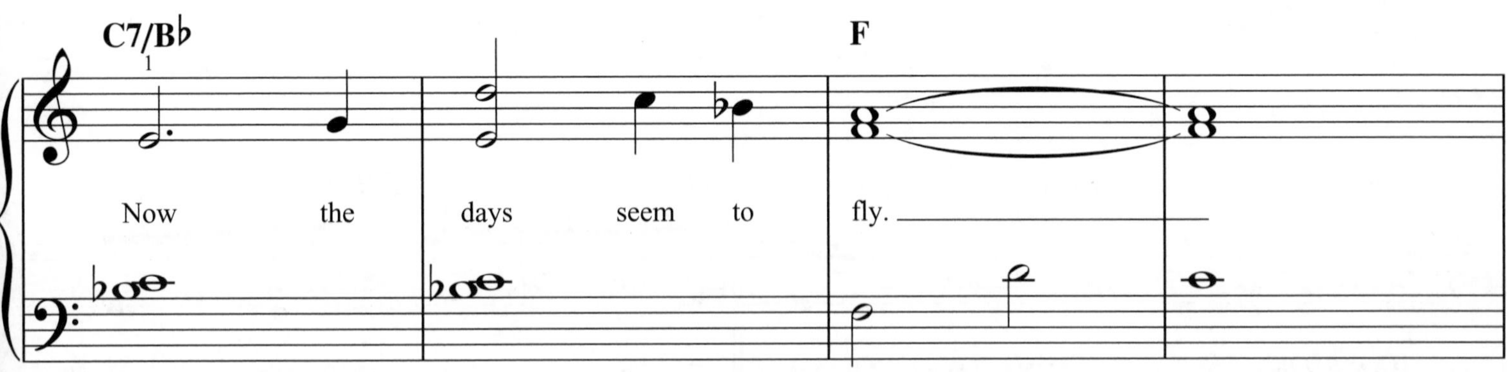
C7/B♭
F
Now the days seem to fly.

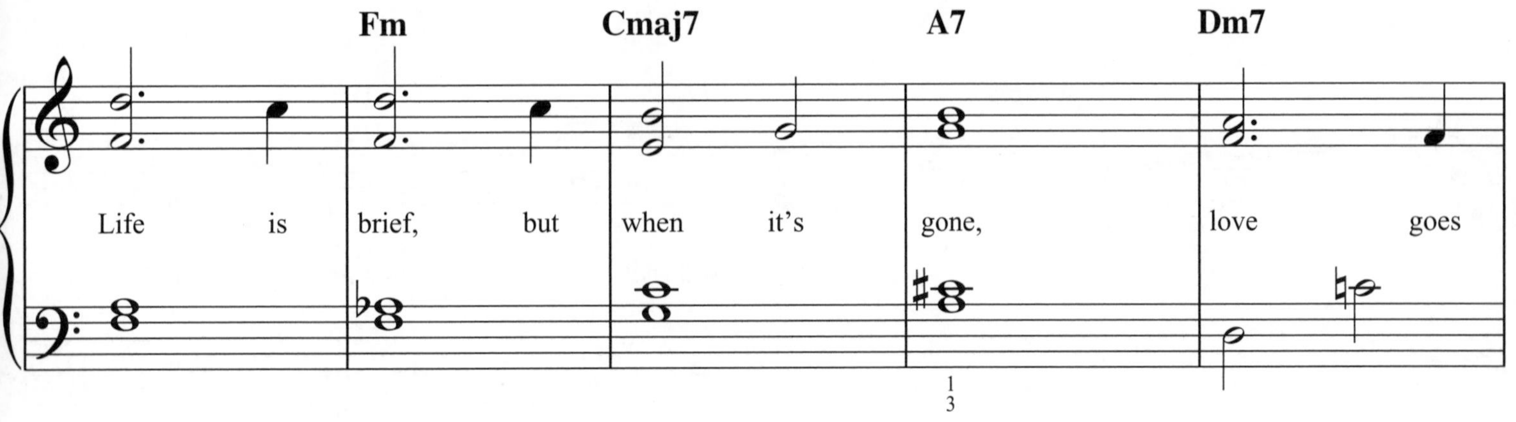
Fm
Cmaj7
A7
Dm7
Life is brief, but when it's gone, love goes

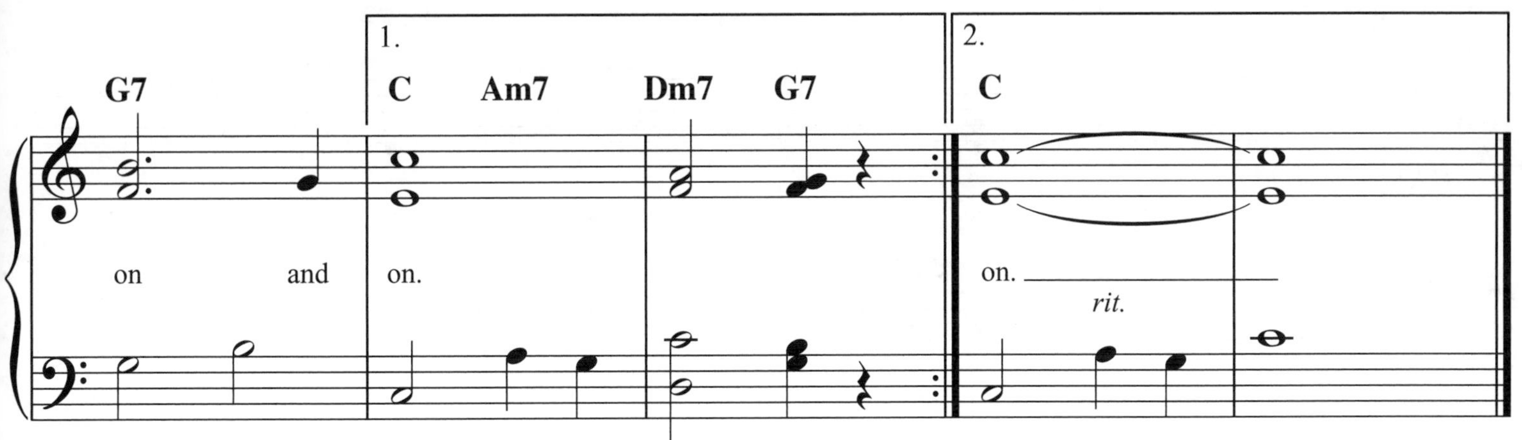
G7
1.
C
Am7
Dm7
G7
2.
C
on and on.
on.
rit.

LOVE IS AN OPEN DOOR

from FROZEN

Music and Lyrics by KRISTEN ANDERSON-LOPEZ
and ROBERT LOPEZ

D/G
A7sus
D
D/F♯
find my own place. And may - be it's the par - ty talk - ing, or the
Em7
A7sus
Bm
cho - c'late fon - due. But with you, (But with you,) I found my
D
E7
place, (I see your face.) and it's noth - ing like I've ev - er known be -
Gm7
D
D/F♯
fore. Love is an o - pen door.

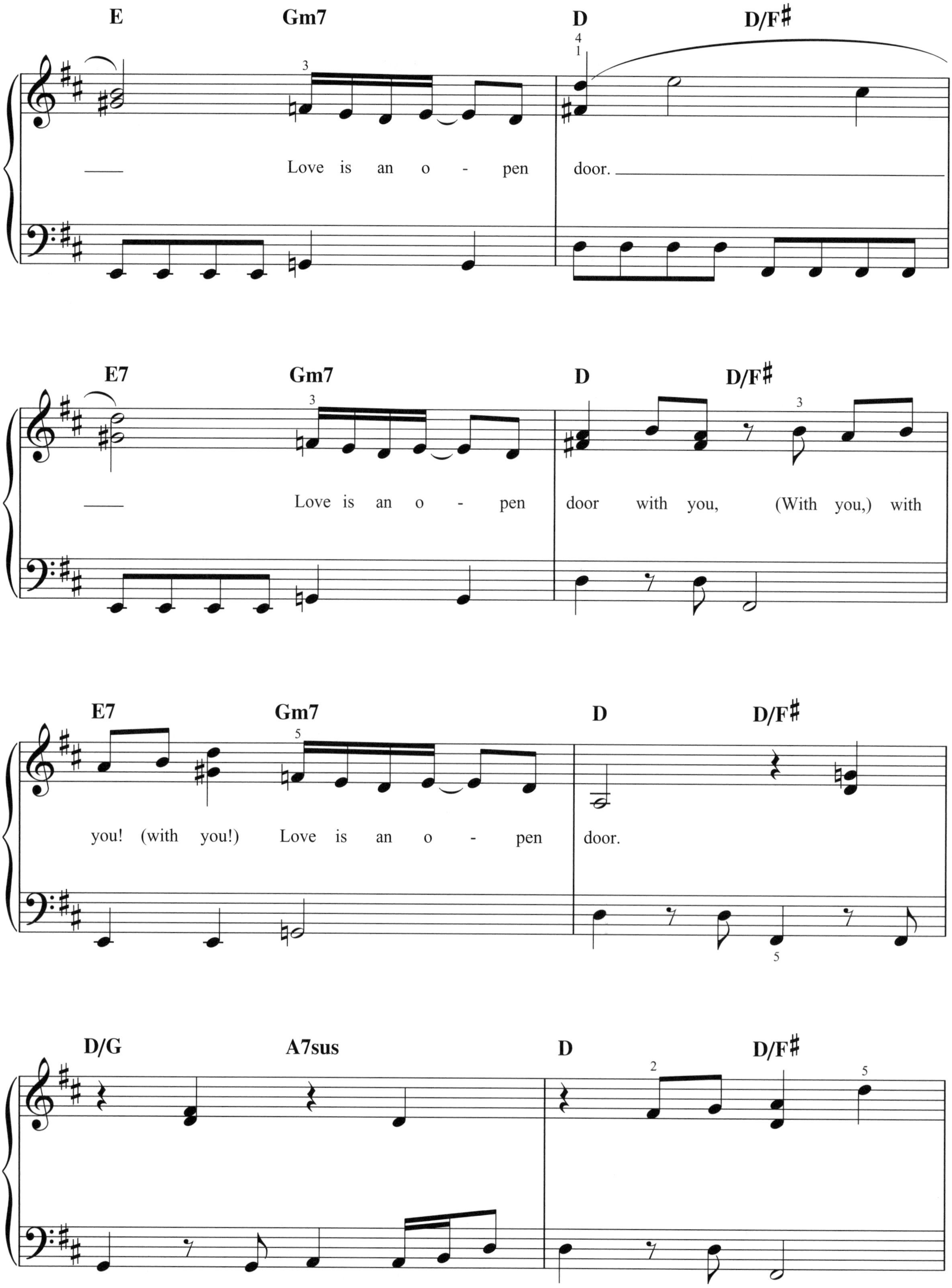

E Gm7 D D/F♯

Love is an o - pen door.

E7 Gm7 D D/F♯

Love is an o - pen door with you, (With you,) with

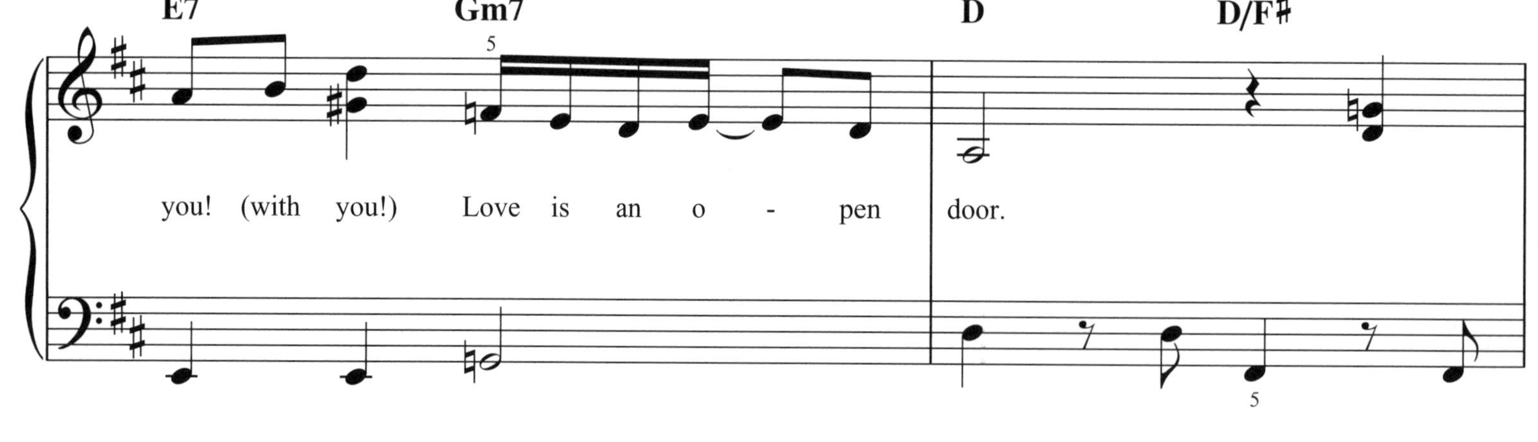

D/G A7sus D D/F♯
I mean, it's cra - zy! We fin - ish each oth - er's...
G A7sus D D/F♯
(sand - wich - es!) That's what I was gonna say! I nev - er met some - one who thinks so much like
Em7 A7sus D D/F♯
me. Jinx! Jinx a - gain! Our men - tal syn - chro - ni - za - tion can
G A7sus D D/F♯
have but one ex - pla - na - tion: You and I were just meant to be.

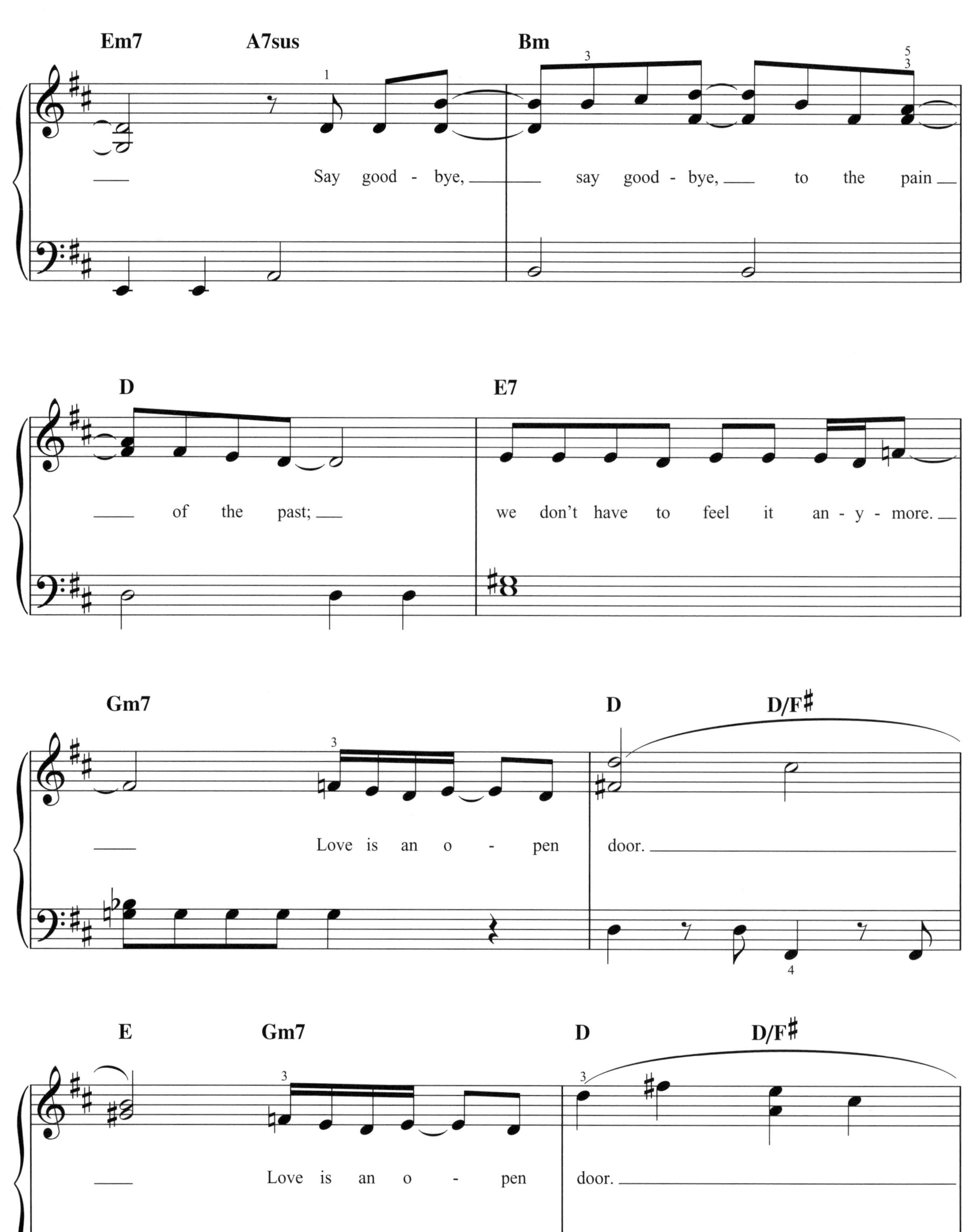
Em7
A7sus
Bm
Say good - bye,
say good - bye,
to the pain
D
E7
of the past;
we don't have to feel it an - y - more.
Gm7
D
D/F♯
Love is an o - pen
door.
E
Gm7
D
D/F♯
Love is an o - pen
door.

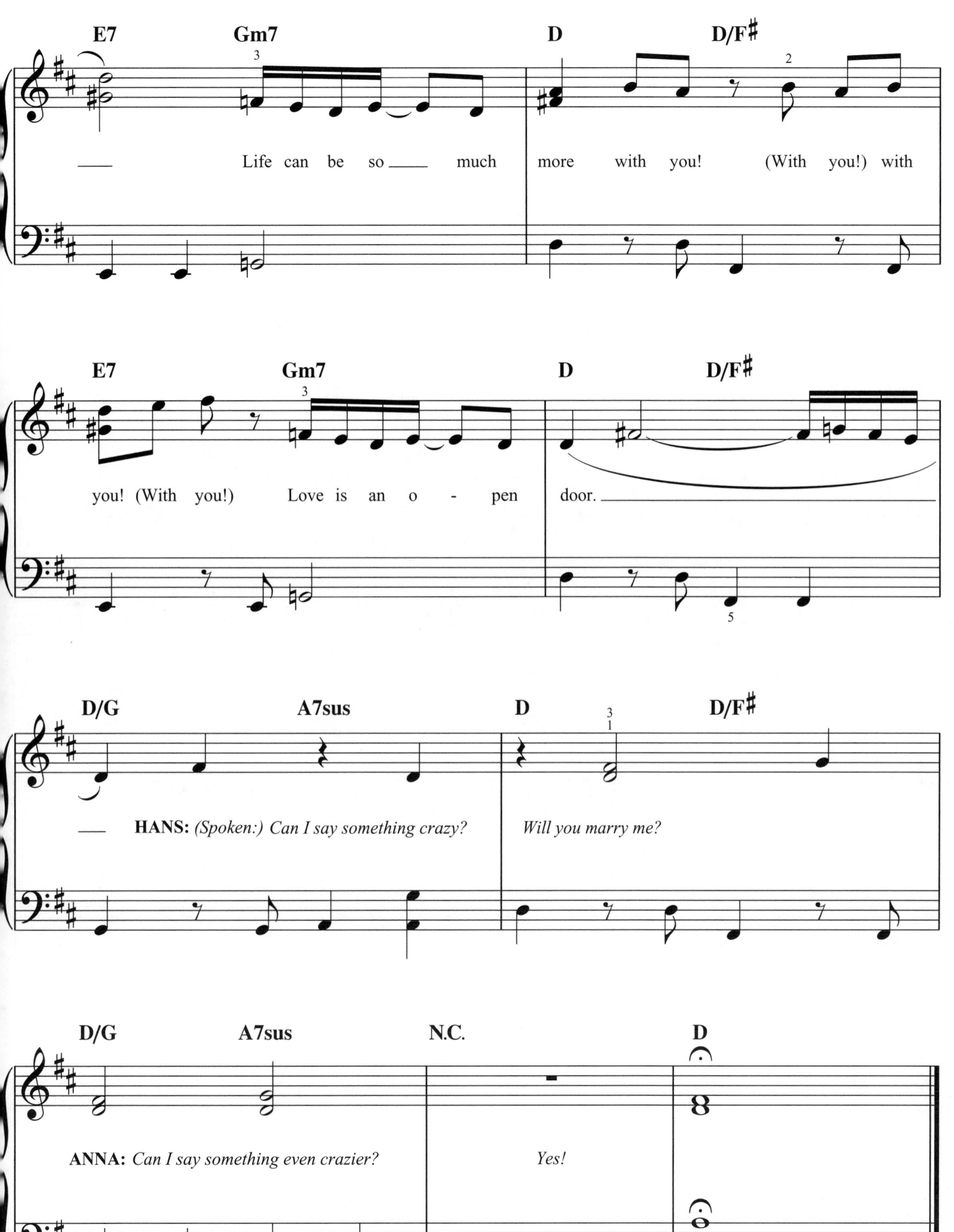
E7
Gm7
D
D/F♯
Life can be so much more with you! (With you!) with
you! (With you!) Love is an o - pen door.
D/G
A7sus
HANS: (Spoken:) Can I say something crazy?
Will you marry me?
N.C.
ANNA: Can I say something even crazier?
Yes!

ONCE UPON A DREAM

from SLEEPING BEAUTY

Words and Music by SAMMY FAIN
and JACK LAWRENCE
Adapted from a Theme by TCHAIKOVSKY

Moderately

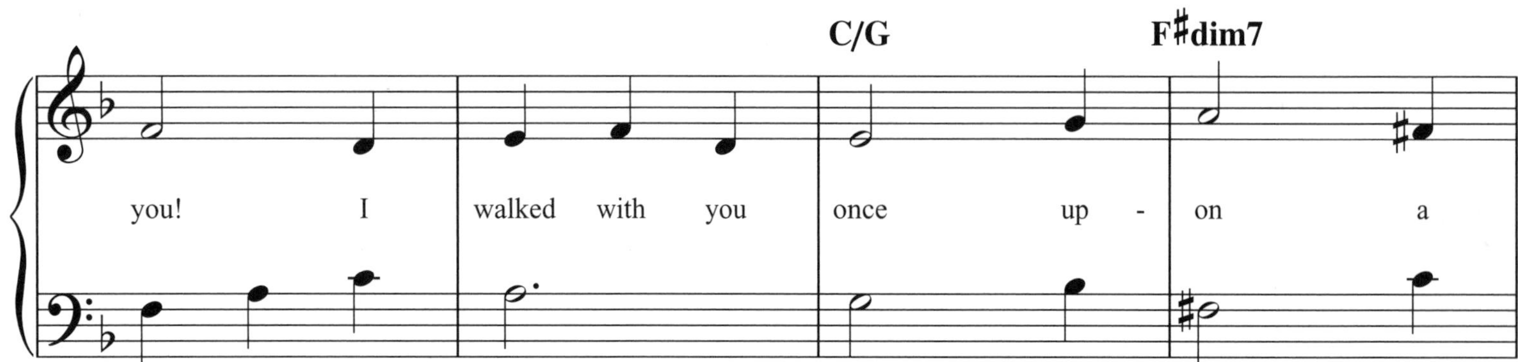

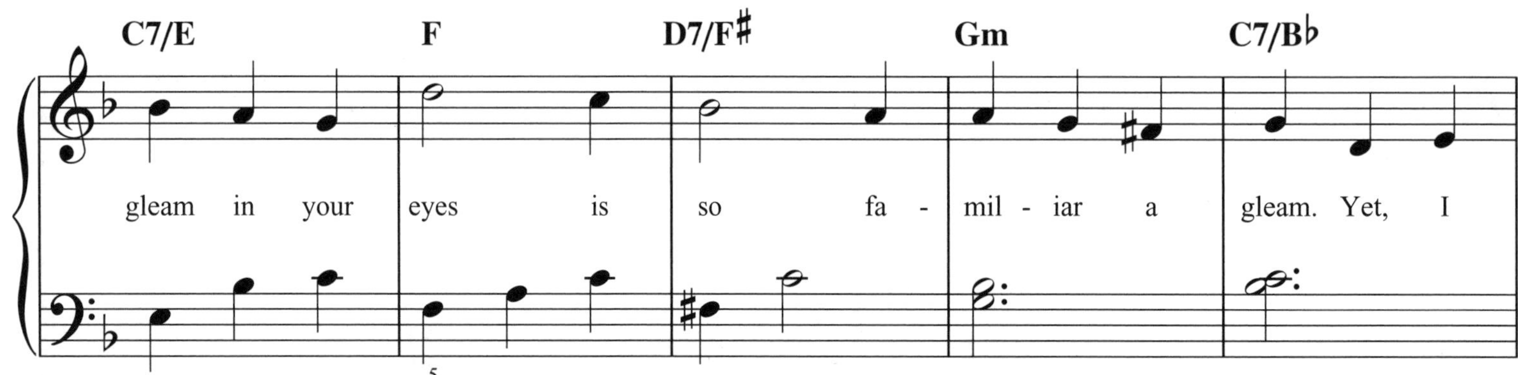

F
Gm
know
it's
true
that
vi - sions
are
sel - dom

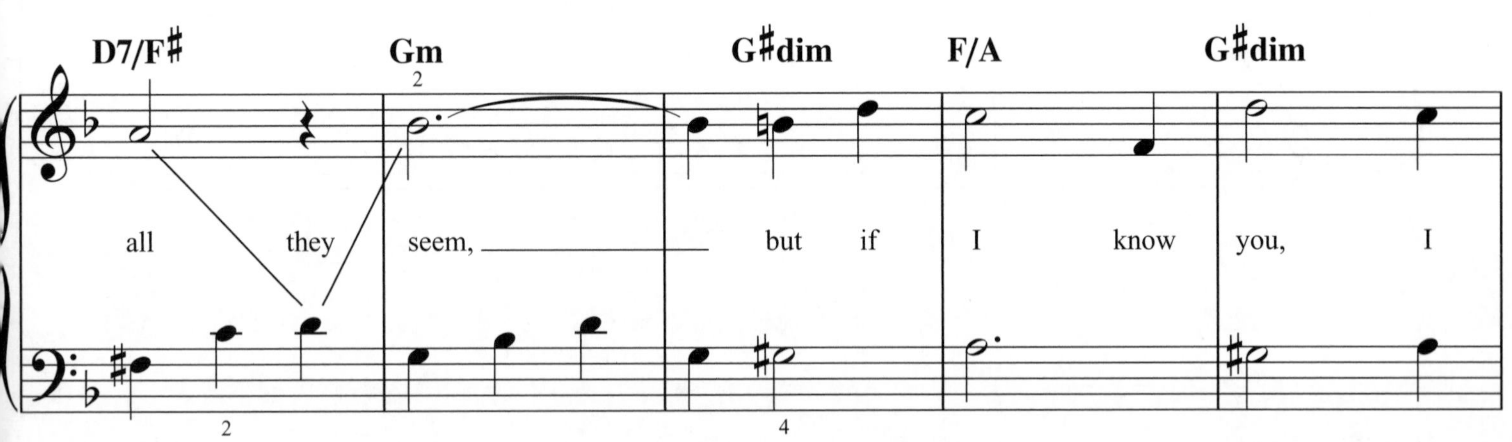
D7/F♯
Gm
G♯dim
F/A
G♯dim
all
they
seem,
but
if
I
know
you,
I

Gm
C7/B♭
F
F♯m
D7/C
know what you'll
do:
you'll
love me at
once
the
way you did

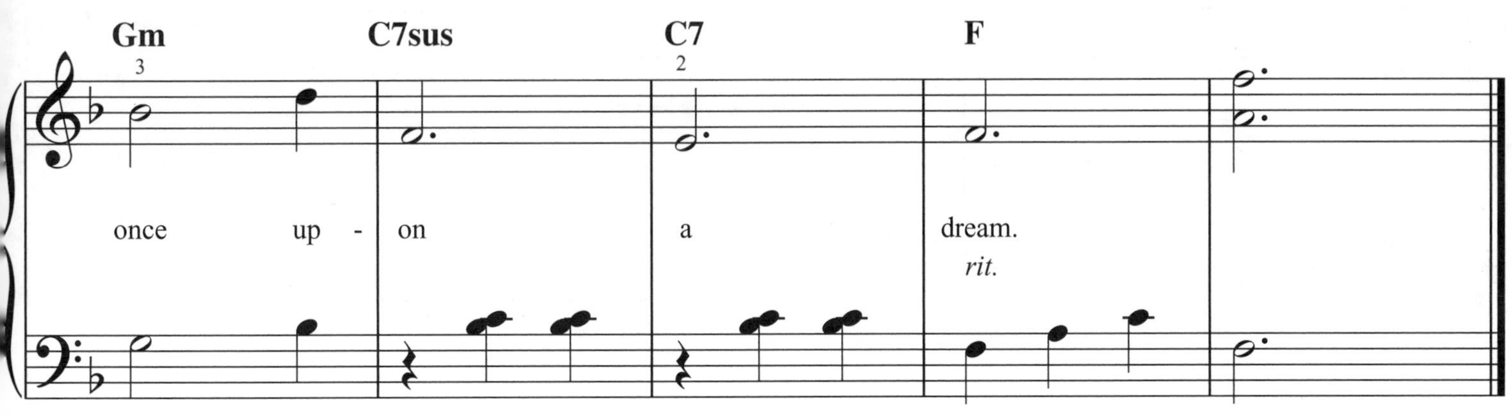
Gm
C7sus
C7
F
once
up -
on
a
dream.
rit.

SO THIS IS LOVE

from CINDERELLA

Words and Music by MACK DAVID,
AL HOFFMAN and JERRY LIVINGSTON

Tenderly

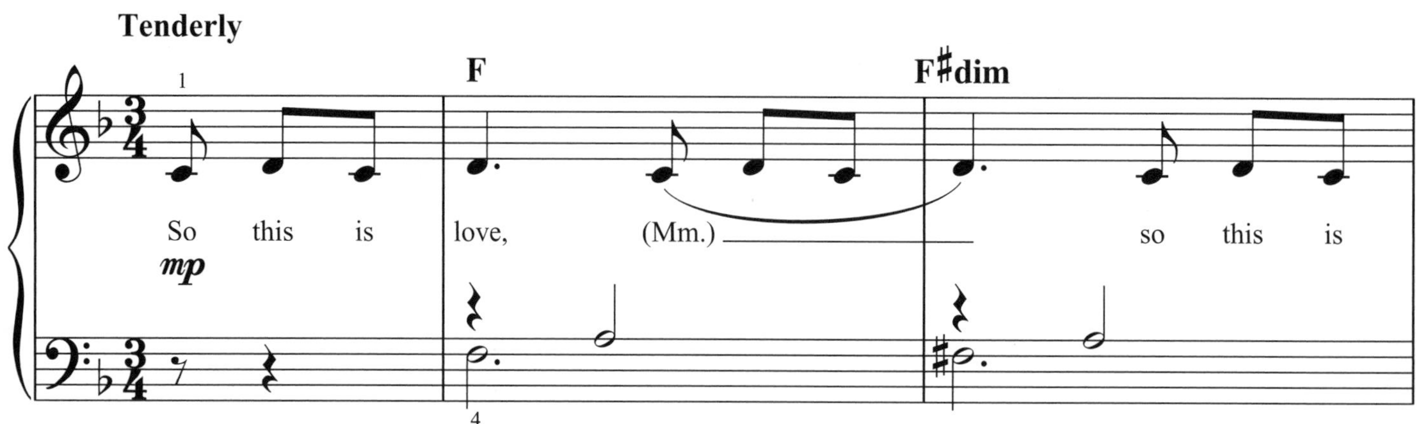

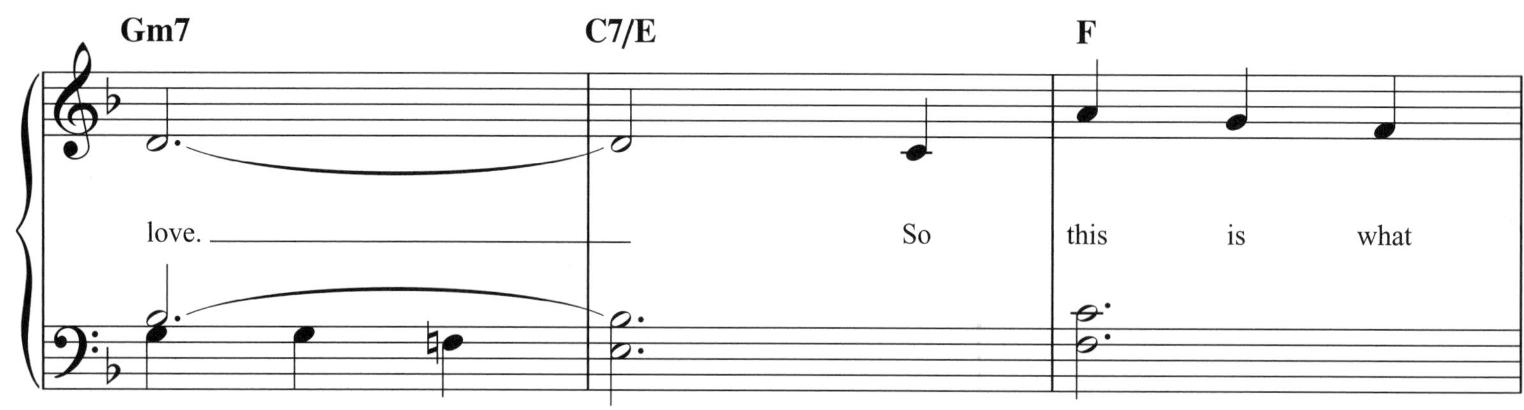

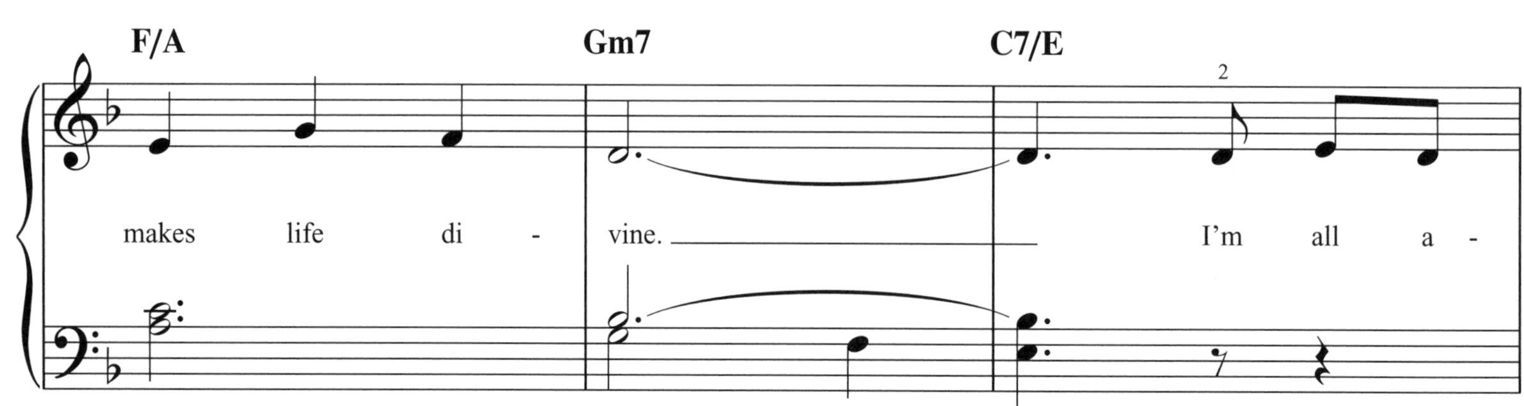

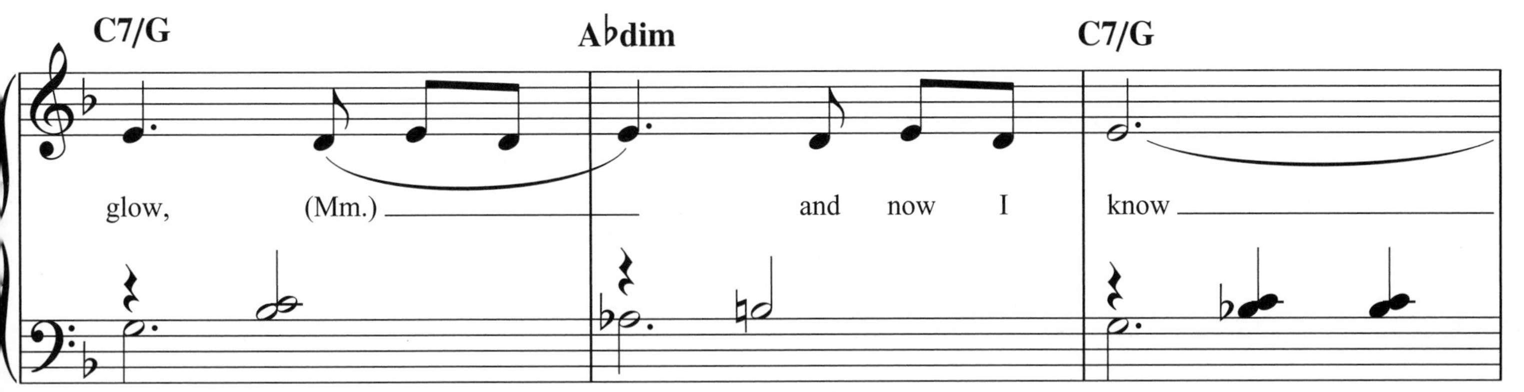
C7/G
A♭dim
C7/G
glow, (Mm.)
and now I
know

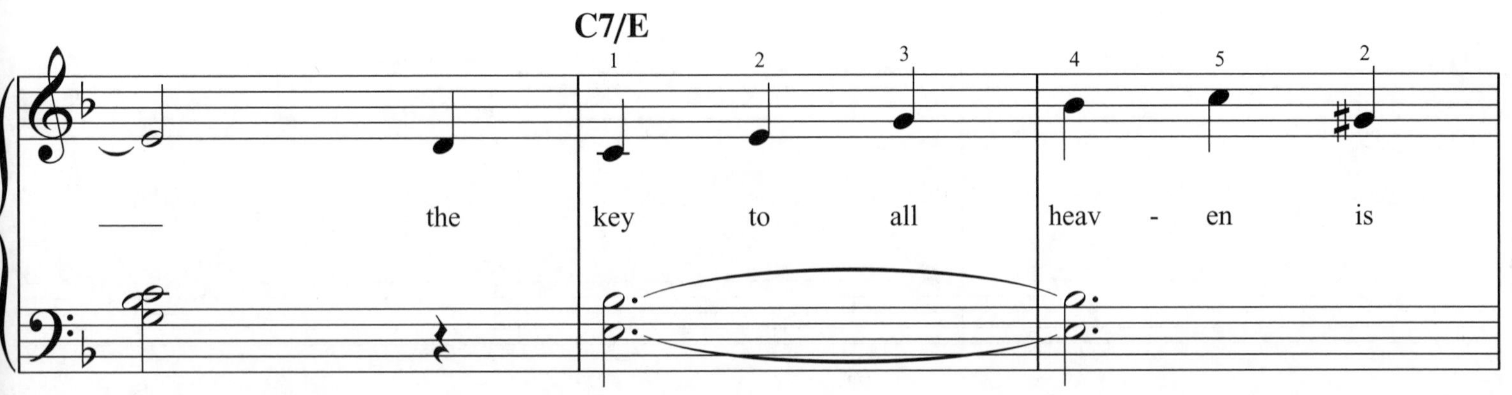
C7/E
the
key to all
heav - en is

F
mine.
My heart has
wings, (Mm.)

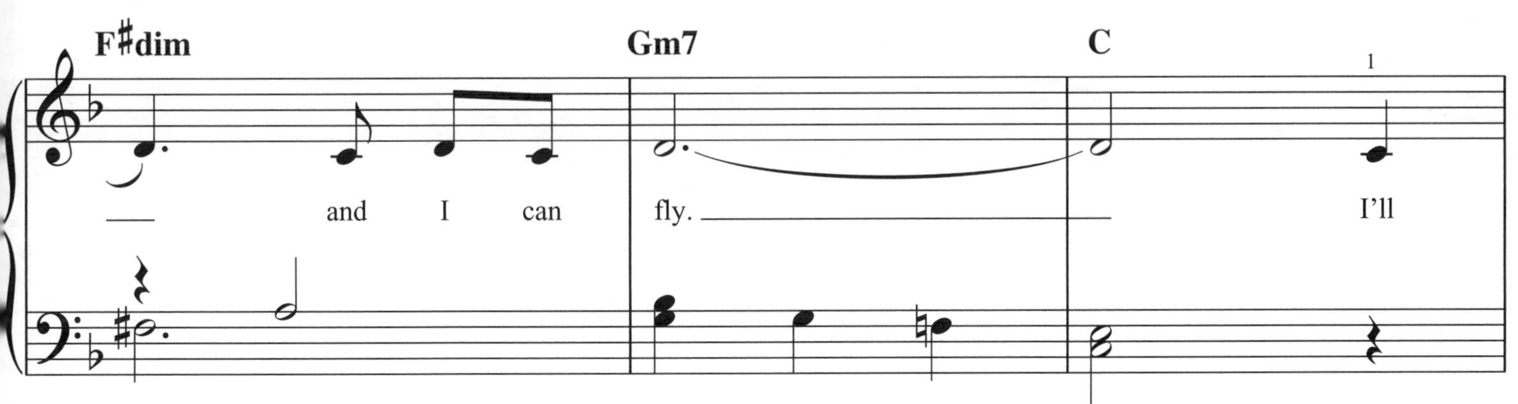
F♯dim
Gm7
C
and I can
fly.
I'll

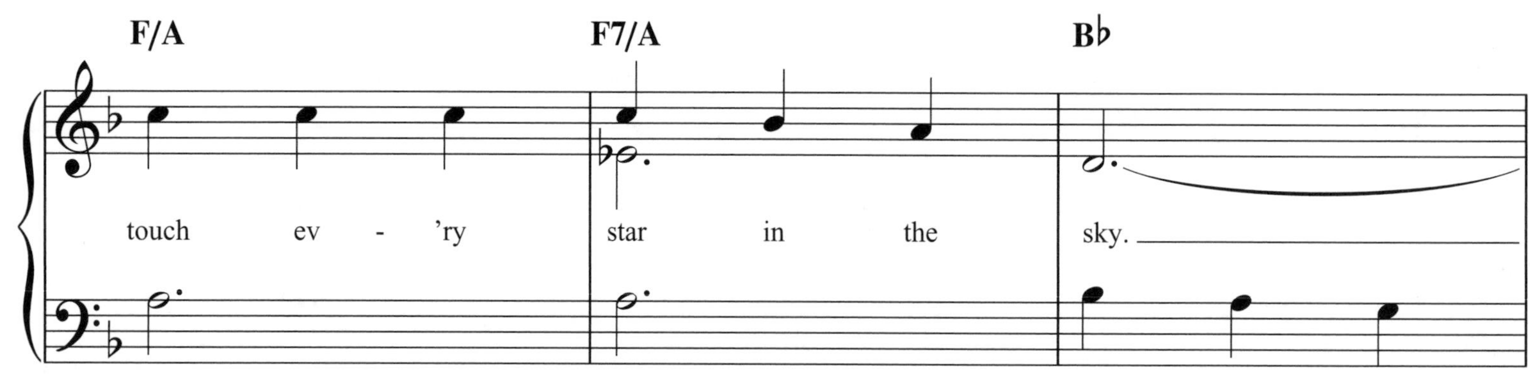
F/A
F7/A
B♭
touch ev - 'ry
star in the
sky.

Gm7
C7
2
1
So
this is the
mir - a - cle that

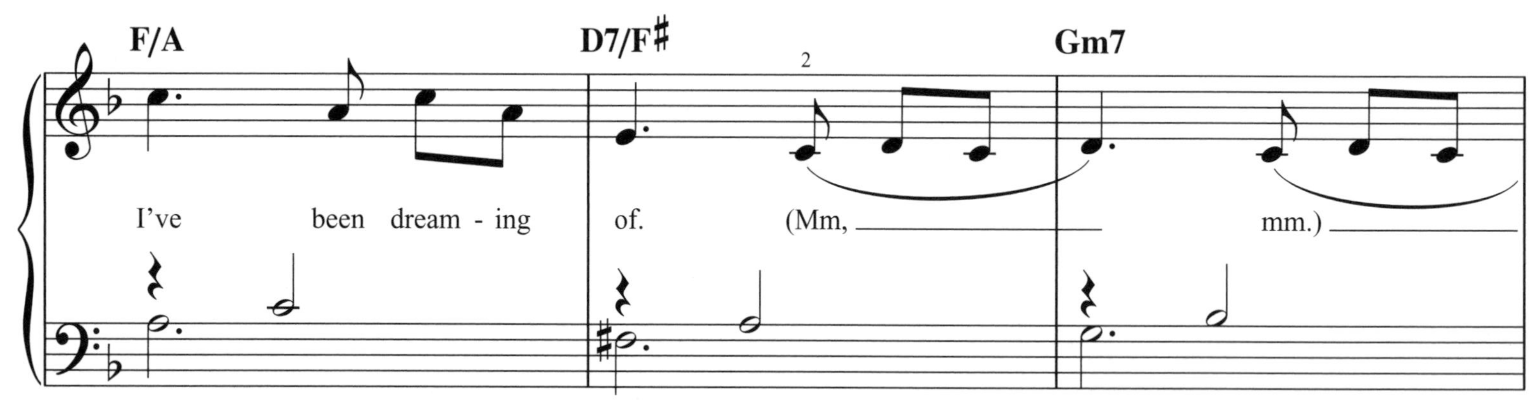
F/A
D7/F♯
Gm7
2
I've been dream - ing
of. (Mm,
mm.)

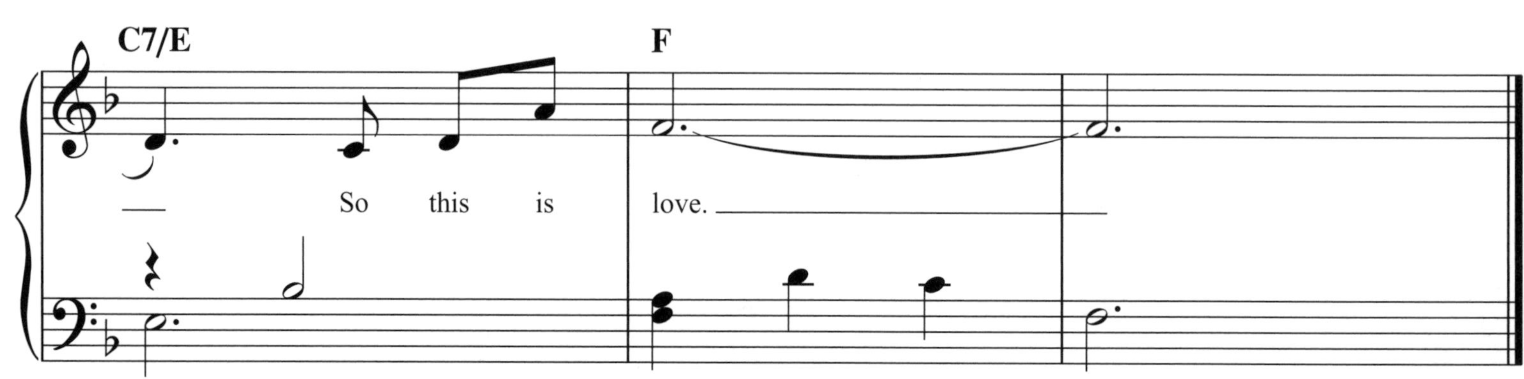
C7/E
F
So this is
love.

SOME DAY MY PRINCE WILL COME

from SNOW WHITE AND THE SEVEN DWARFS

Words by LARRY MOREY
Music by FRANK CHURCHILL

Slow Waltz

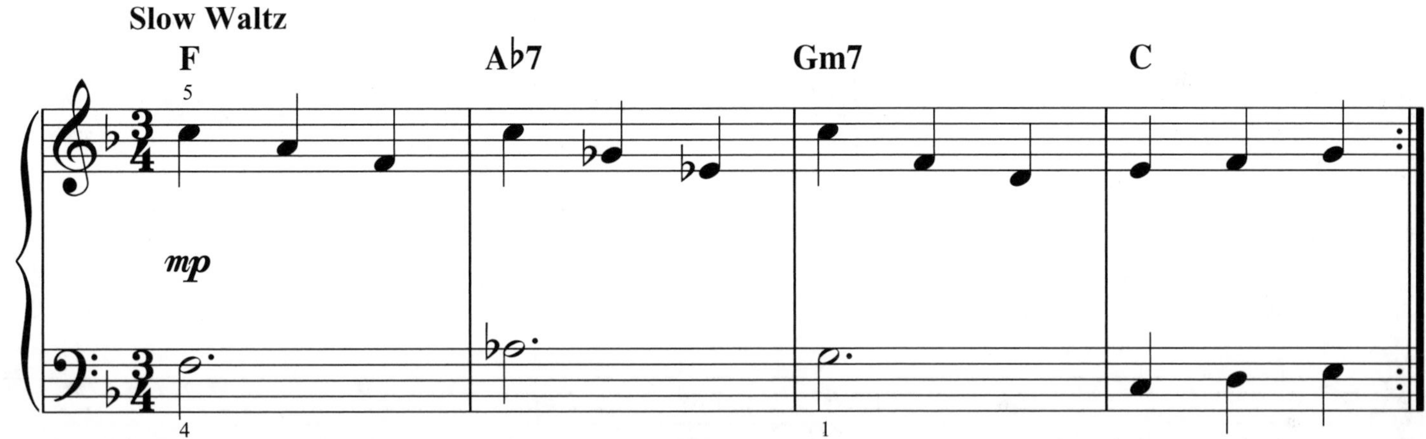

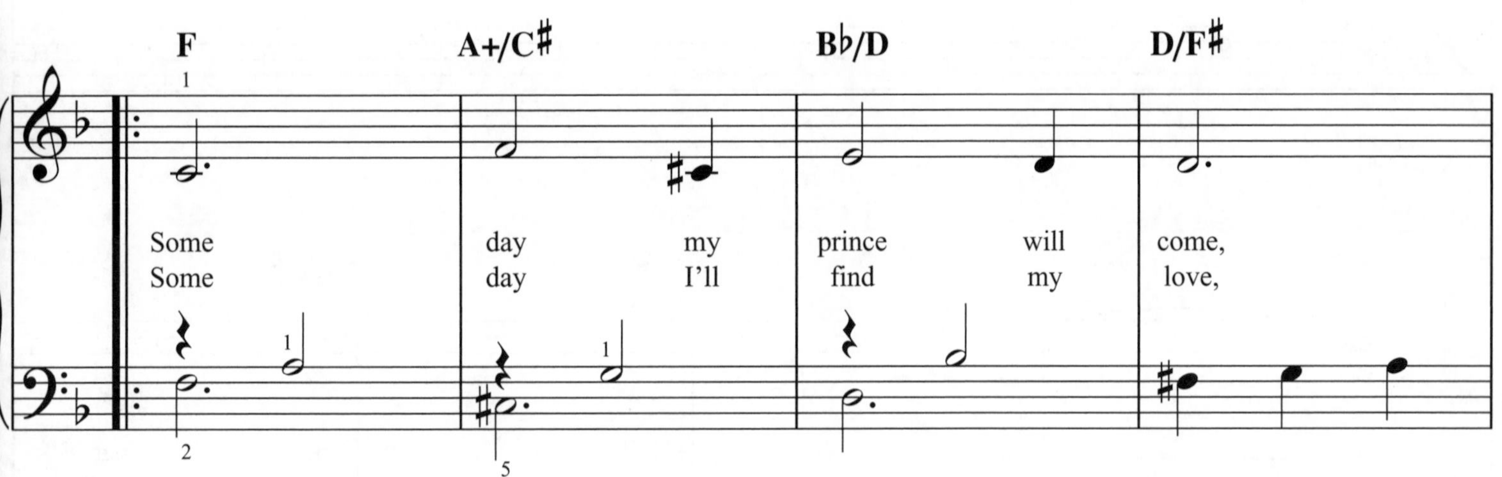

F/A
E/G♯
Gm7
thrill - ing that mo - ment will be,
know her the mo - ment we meet,

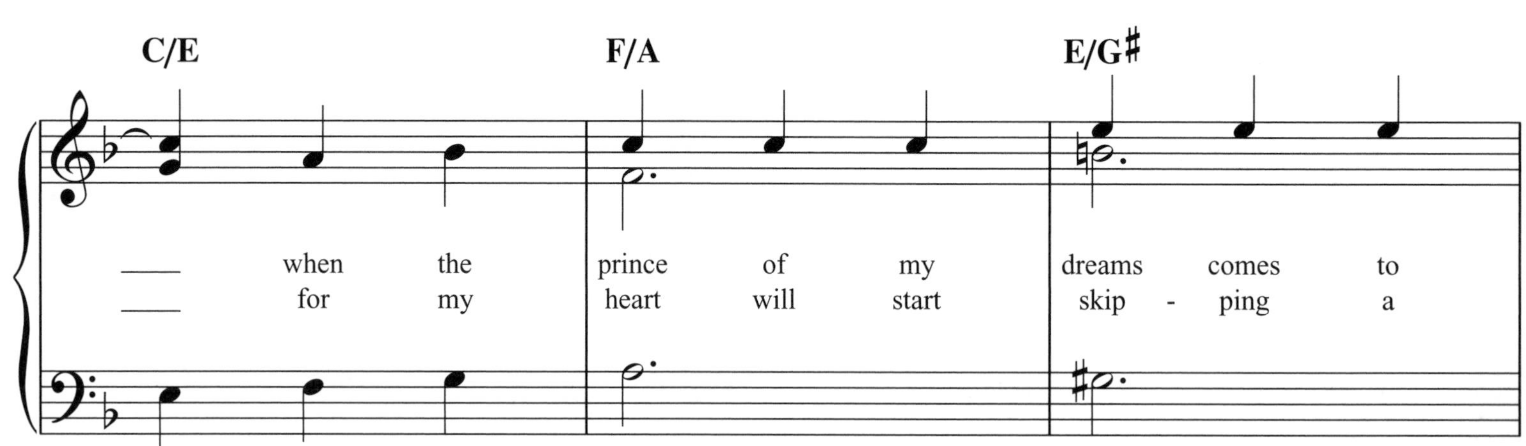
C/E
F/A
E/G♯
when the prince of my dreams comes to
for my heart will start skip - ping a

Gm7
C
F
A+/C♯
me. He'll whis - per
beat. Some day we'll

B♭/D
D/F♯
Gm
B♭/F
"I love you" and steal a
say and do things we've been

C7/E
F
A7/C♯
kiss or two. Though he's
long - ing to. Though she's
far a - way, I'll

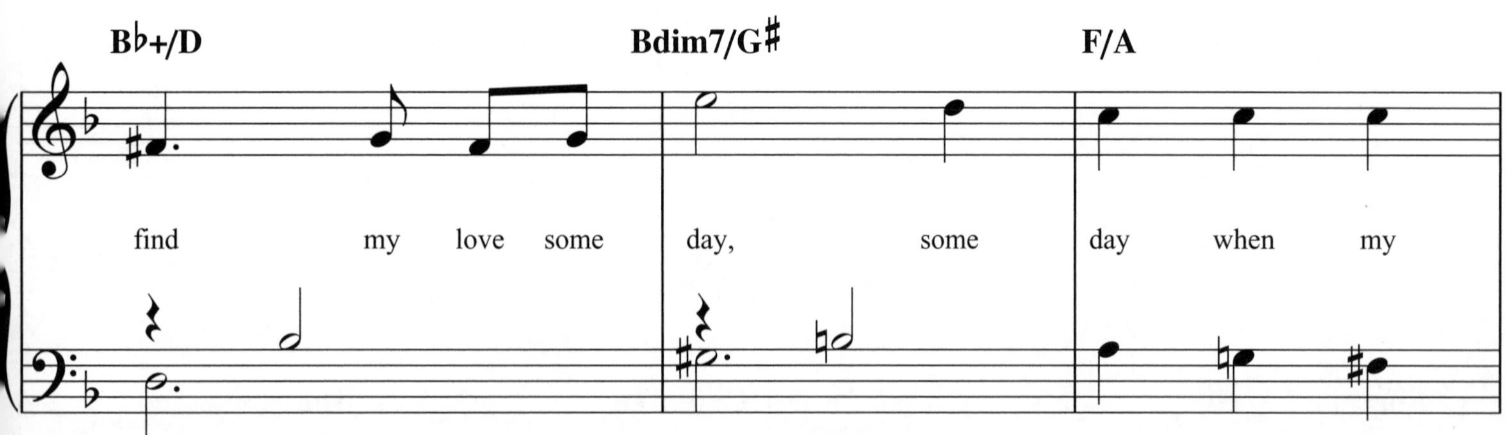
B♭+/D
Bdim7/G♯
F/A
find my love some day, some day when my

Gm7
C
1.
F
A♭7
Gm7
C
2.
F
dreams come true.
true.

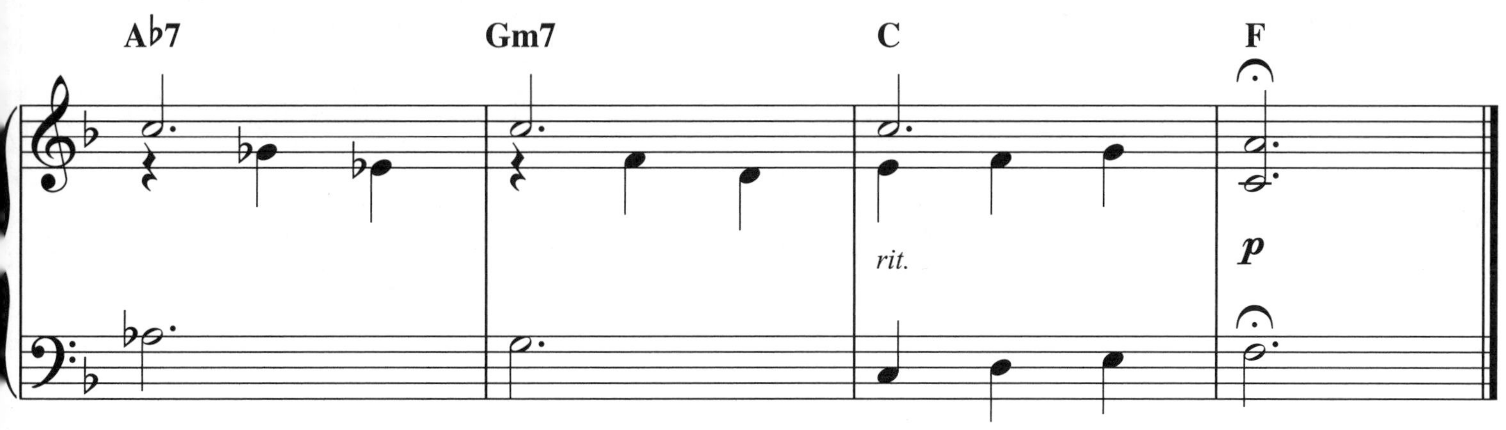
A♭7
Gm7
C
F
rit.
p

TRUE LOVE'S KISS

from ENCHANTED

Music by ALAN MENKEN
Lyrics by STEPHEN SCHWARTZ

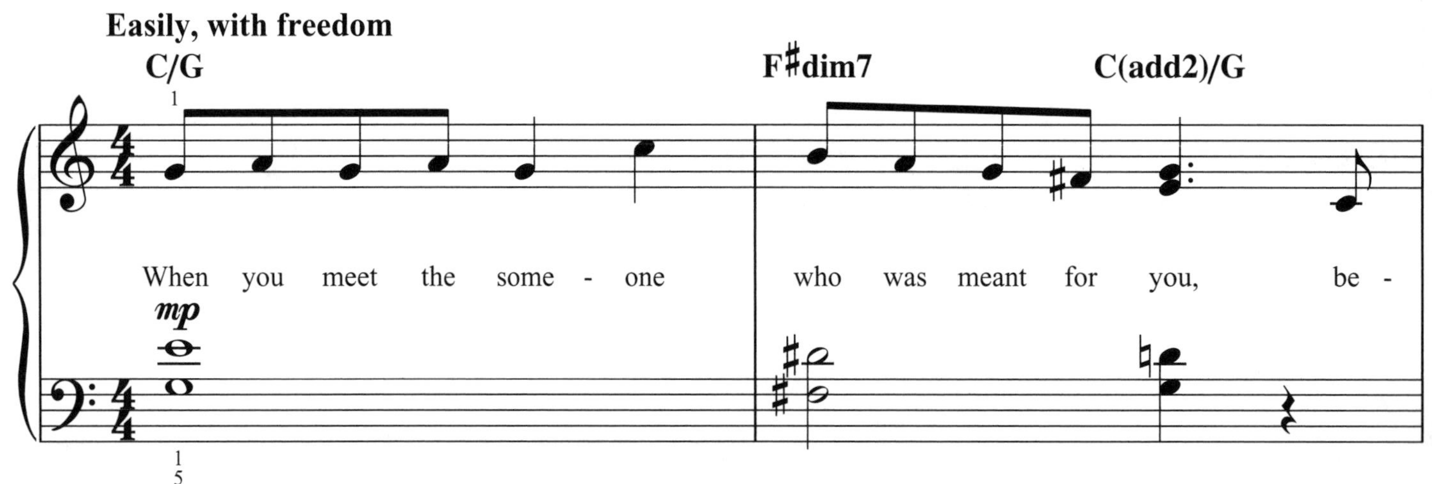

More flowing, still freely
Am7 D G7sus G7 C Em F C(add2)
ev - 'ry - bod - y needs. I've been dream - ing of a true love's kiss;

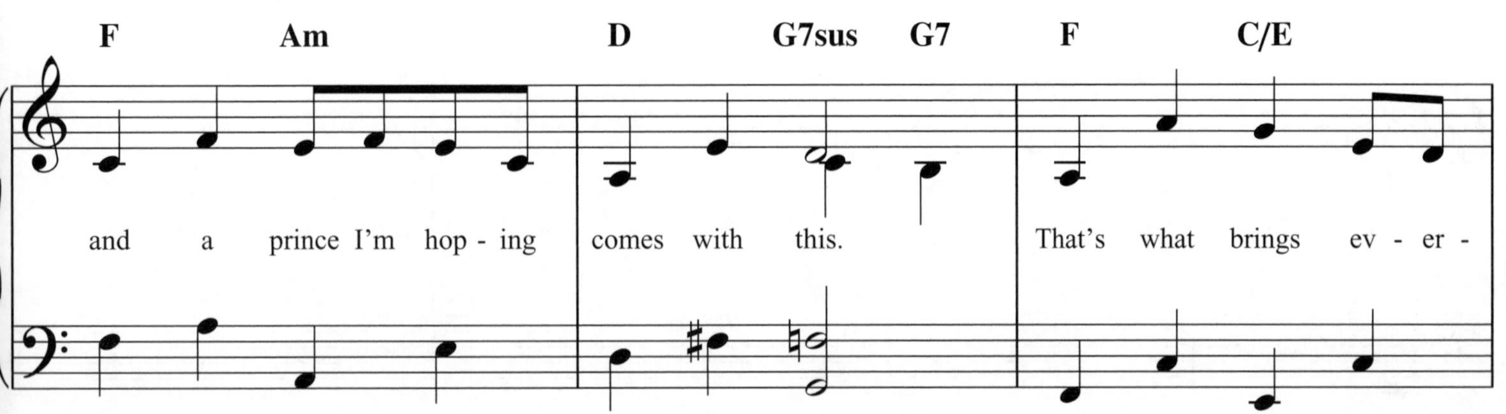
F Am D G7sus G7 F C/E
and a prince I'm hop - ing comes with this. That's what brings ev - er -

Am7 D F/G G G7
af - ter - ings so hap - py. And

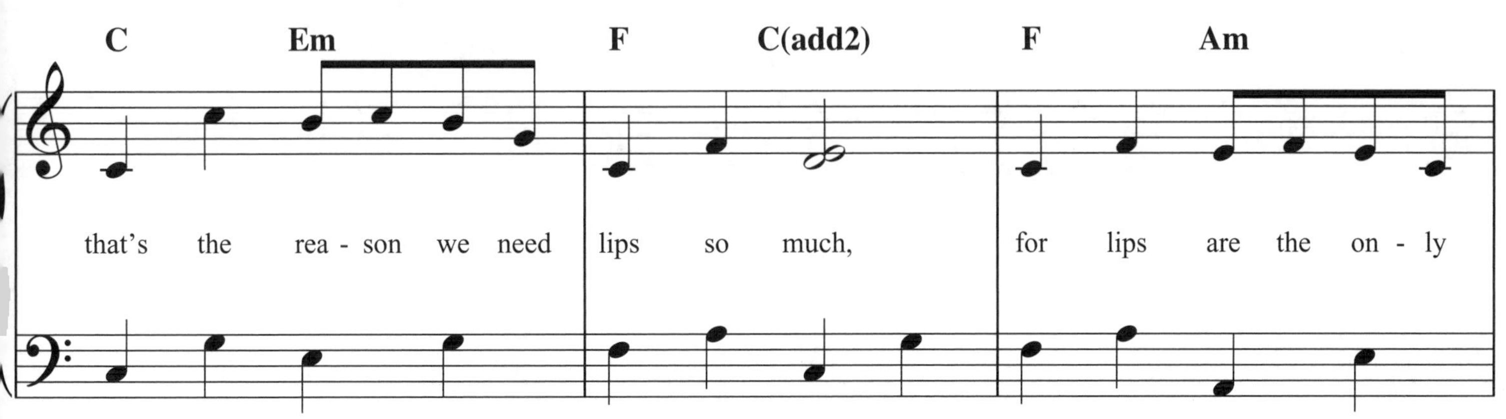
C Em F C(add2) F Am
that's the rea - son we need lips so much, for lips are the on - ly

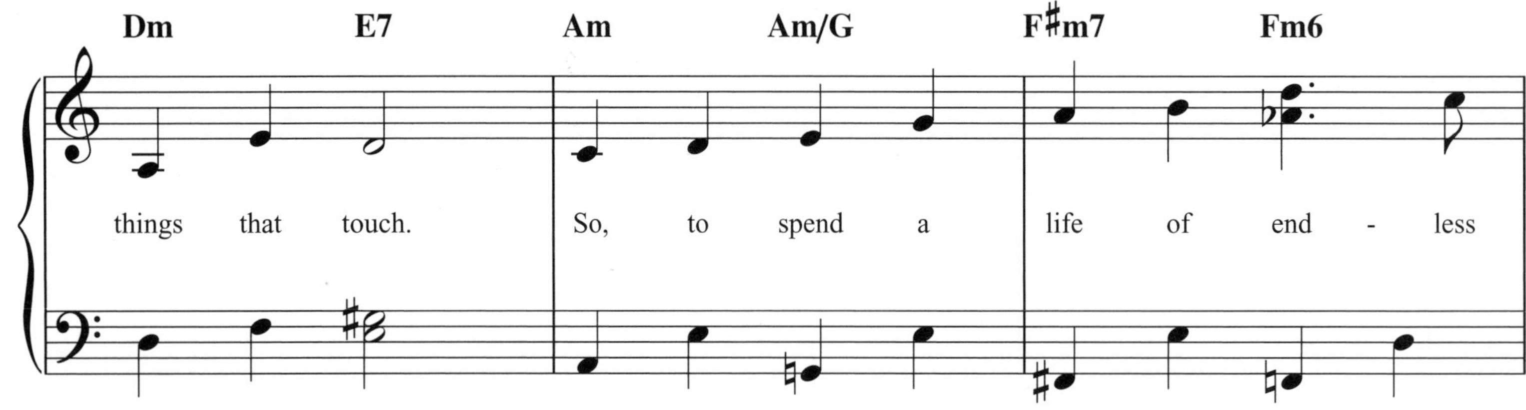
Dm
E7
Am
Am/G
F♯m7
Fm6
things that touch.
So, to spend a life of end - less

C/E
A
Dm7
bliss,
just find who you love through

Fmaj7/G
G7♭9
C
F
C(add2)
true love's kiss.

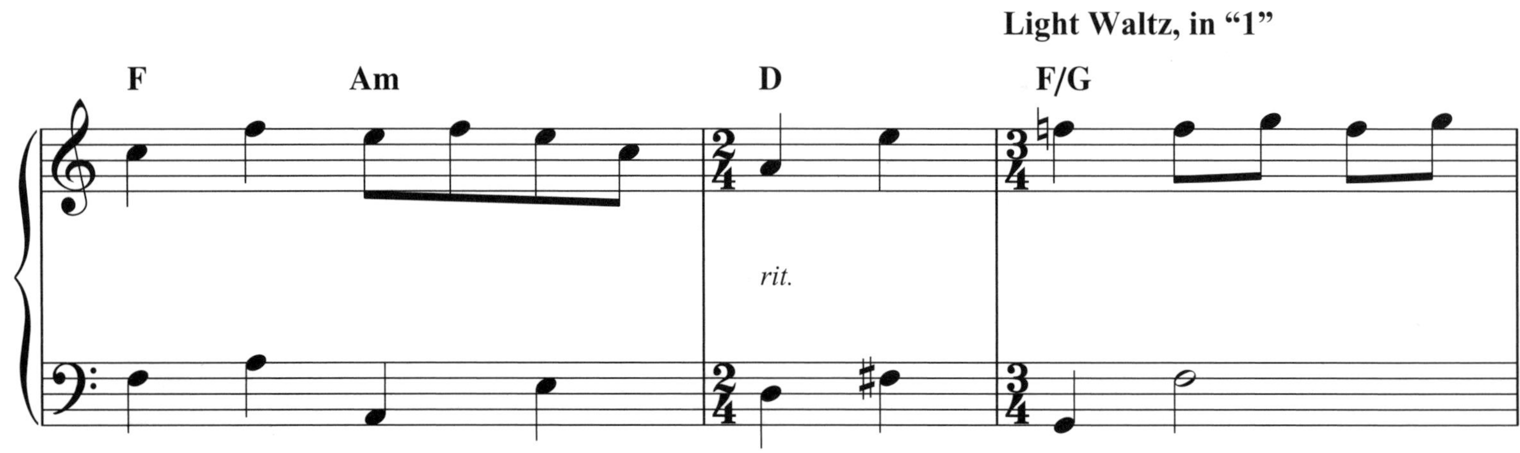
Light Waltz, in "1"
F
Am
D
F/G
rit.

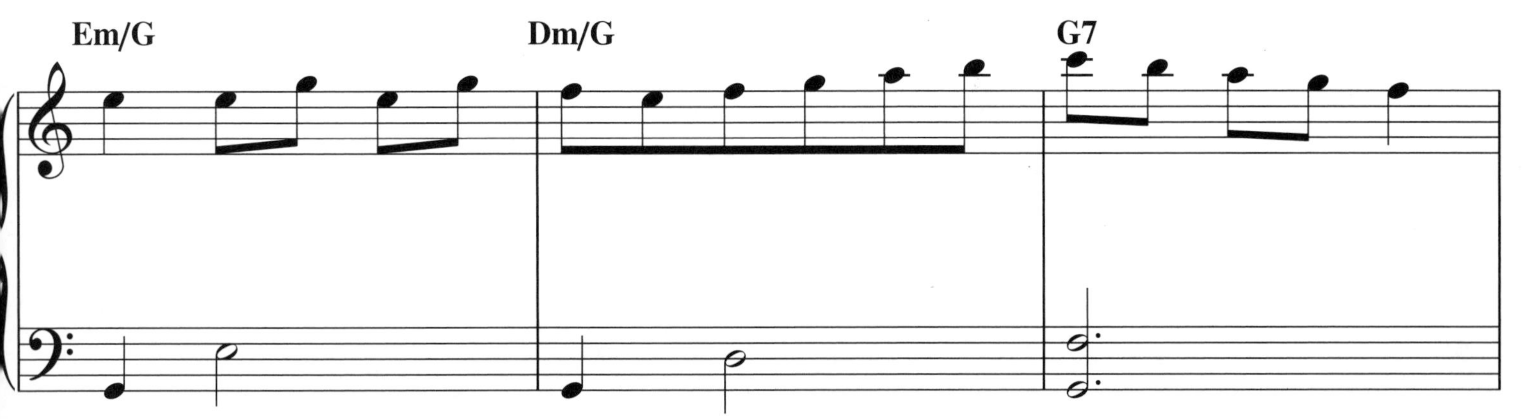
Em/G
Dm/G
G7

C
F♯dim7
Dm7
Ah,
ah,
ah.

G7
E♭
Adim7
Ah,
ah,

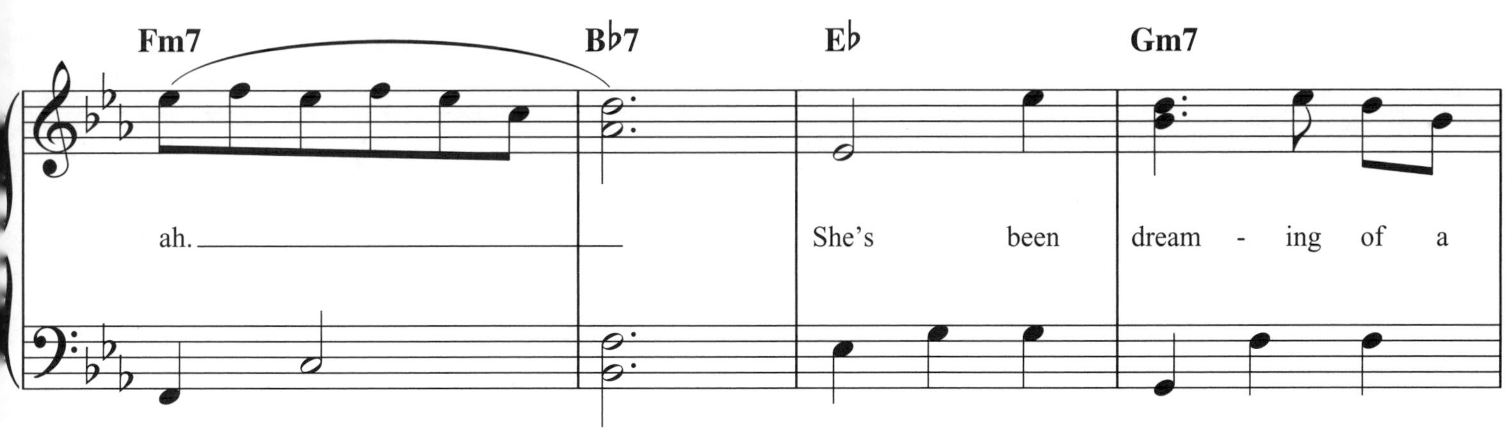
Fm7
B♭7
E♭
Gm7
ah.
She's been dream - ing of a

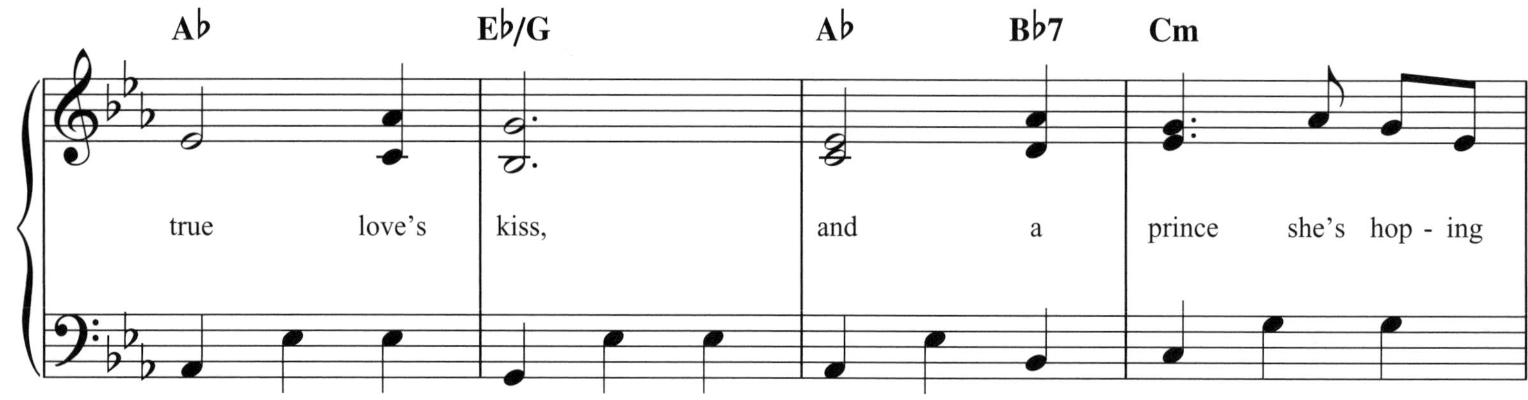
Ab
Eb/G
Ab
Bb7
Cm
true love's kiss, and a prince she's hop - ing

F
Bb7
Ab
Gm7
comes with this. That's what brings ev - er -

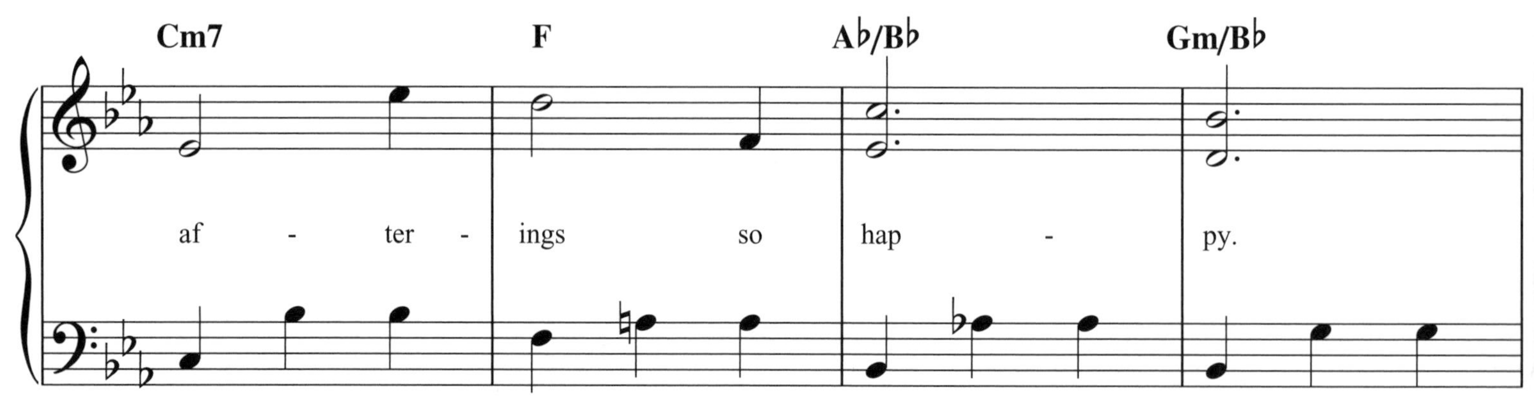
Cm7
F
Ab/Bb
Gm/Bb
af - ter - ings so hap - py.

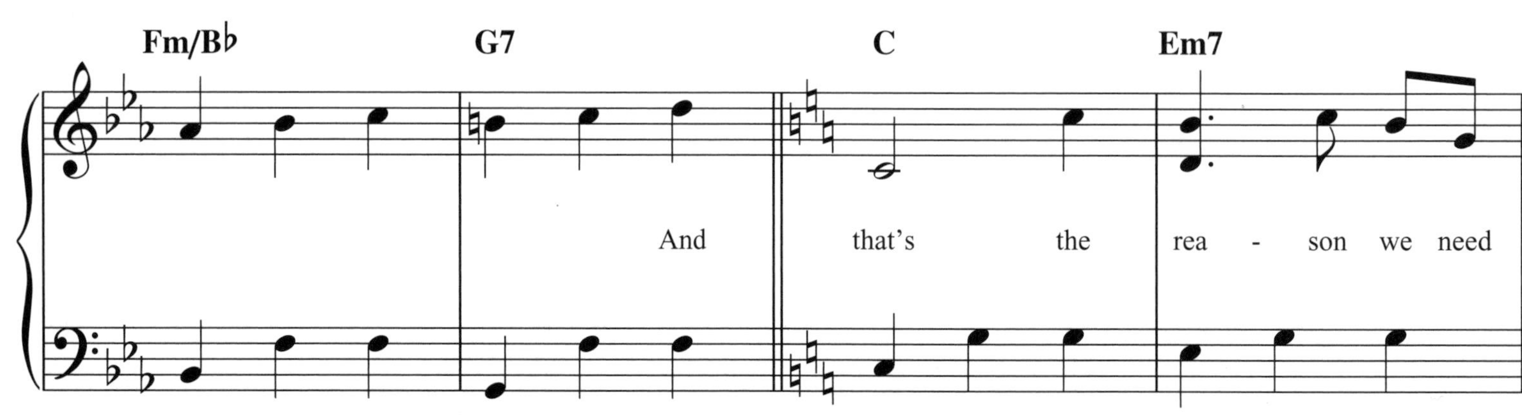
Fm/Bb
G7
C
Em7
And that's the rea - son we need

F
C(add2)
F
G7
Am
lips so much, for lips are the on - ly

D
D9
E7sus
E7
things that touch.
rit.

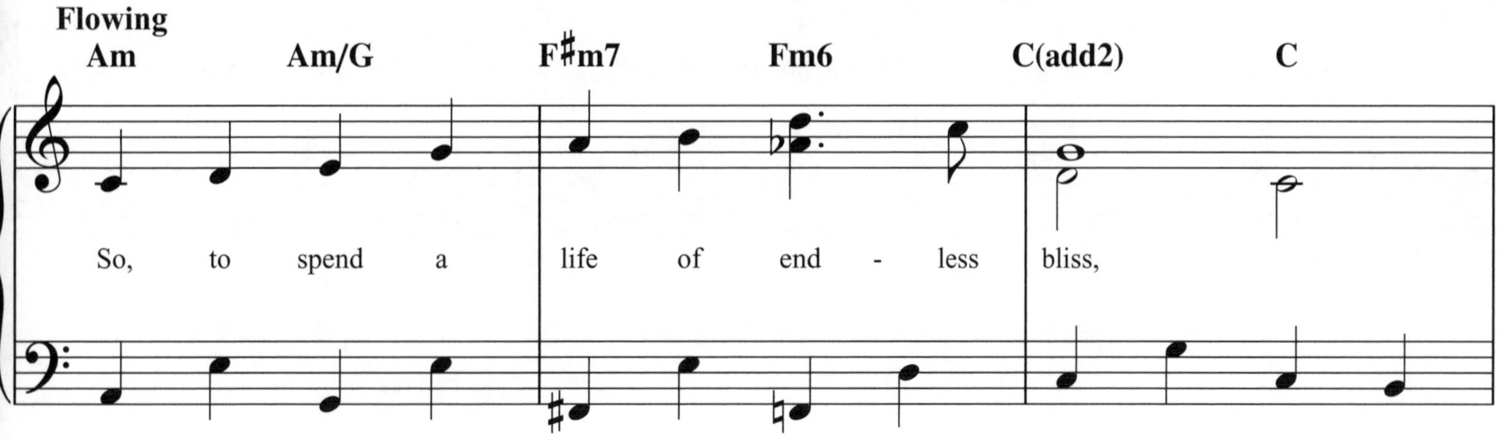
Flowing
Am
Am/G
F♯m7
Fm6
C(add2)
C
So, to spend a life of end - less bliss,

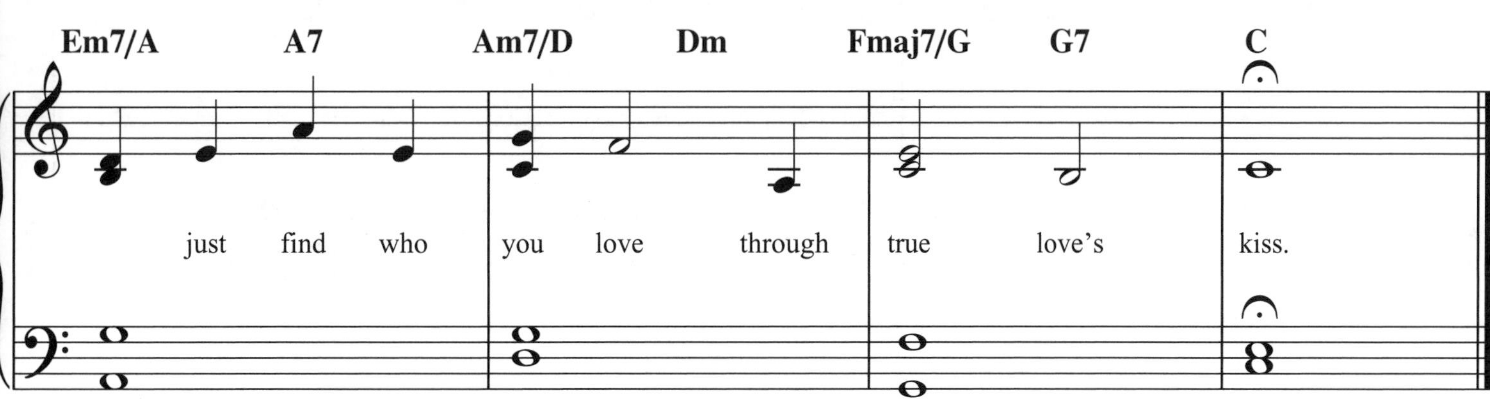
Em7/A
A7
Am7/D
Dm
Fmaj7/G
G7
C
just find who you love through true love's kiss.

WHEN SHE LOVED ME

from TOY STORY 2

Music and Lyrics by
RANDY NEWMAN

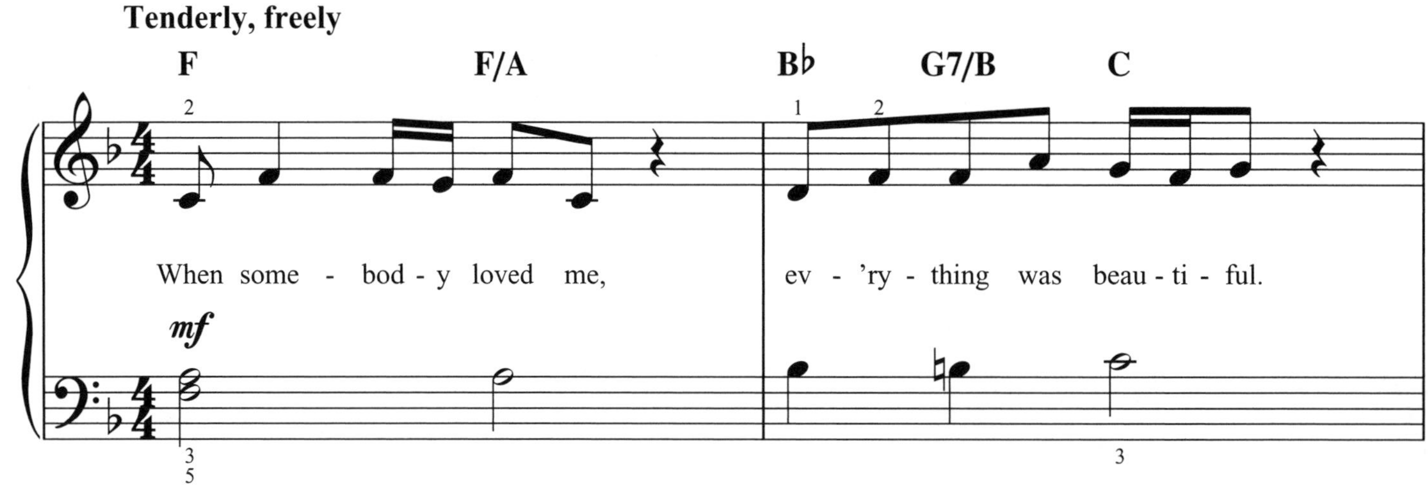

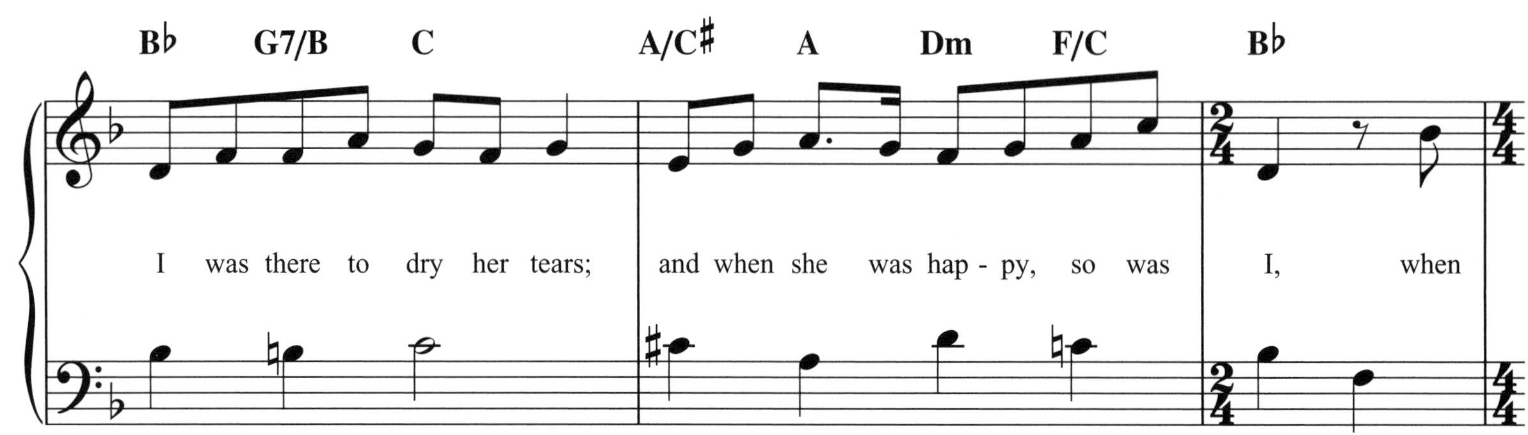

F/C
C/E
F
B♭
C
B♭
she loved me. Through the sum - mer and the fall, we

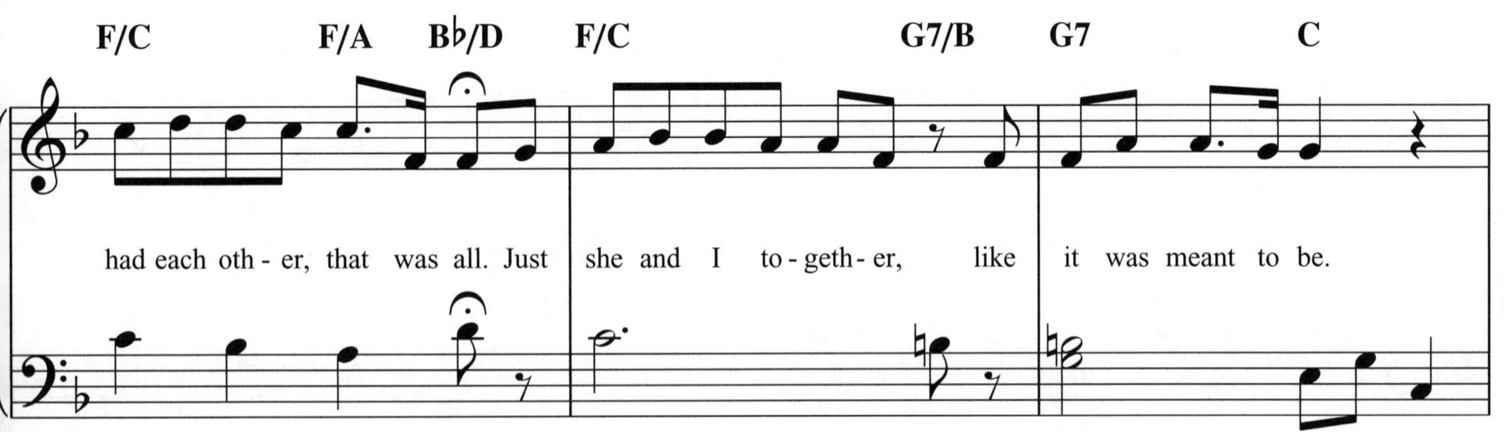
F/C
F/A
B♭/D
F/C
G7/B
G7
C
had each oth - er, that was all. Just she and I to - geth - er, like it was meant to be.

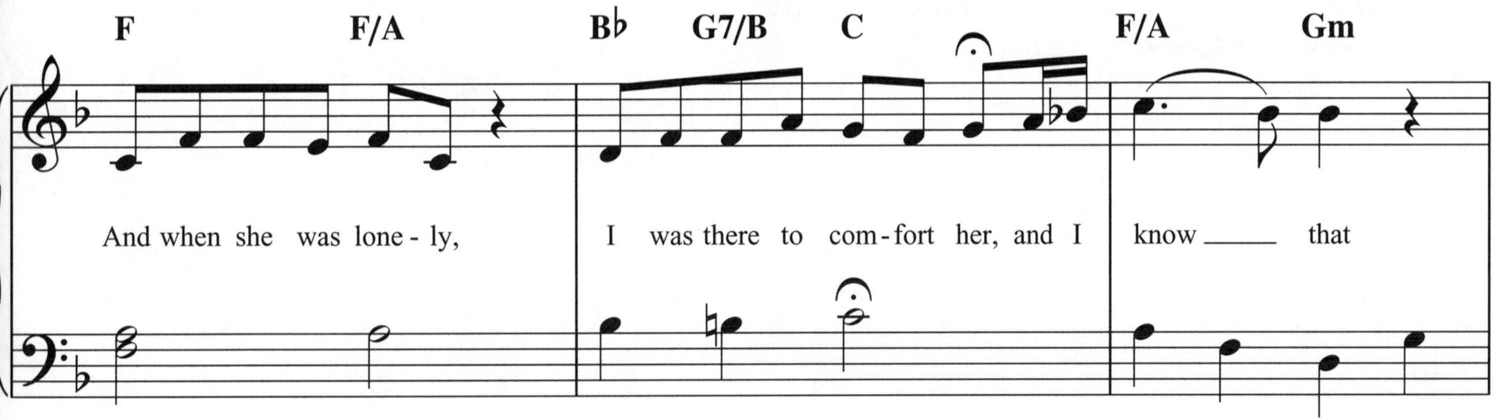
F
F/A
B♭
G7/B
C
F/A
Gm
And when she was lone - ly, I was there to com - fort her, and I know that

F/C
C/E
F
she loved me.

Dm
Bbm/Db
F/C
So the years went by; I stayed the same. But

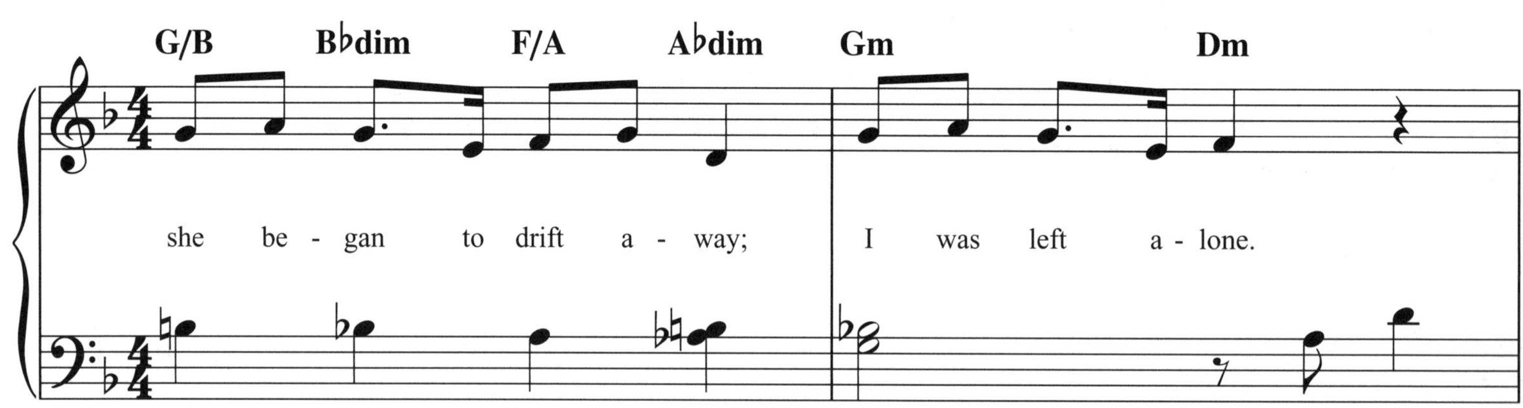
G/B
Bbdim
F/A
Abdim
Gm
Dm
she be - gan to drift a - way; I was left a - lone.

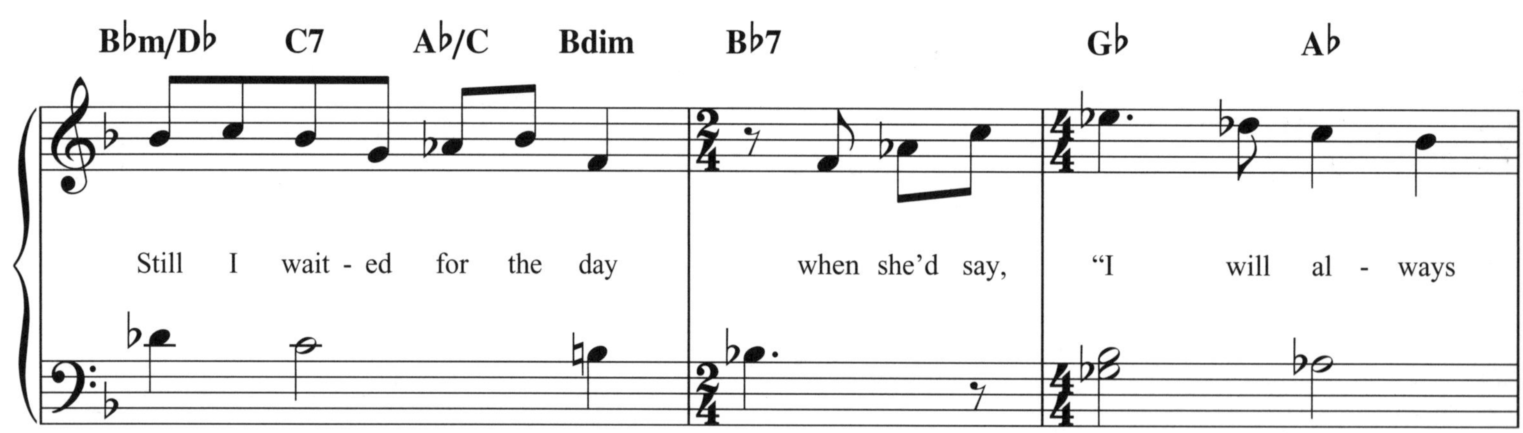
Bbm/Db
C7
Ab/C
Bdim
Bb7
Gb
Ab
Still I wait - ed for the day when she'd say, "I will al - ways

Db/F
C7/E
F
F/A
Bb
G7/B
C
love you." Lone - ly and for - got - ten, nev - er thought she'd look my way, and she

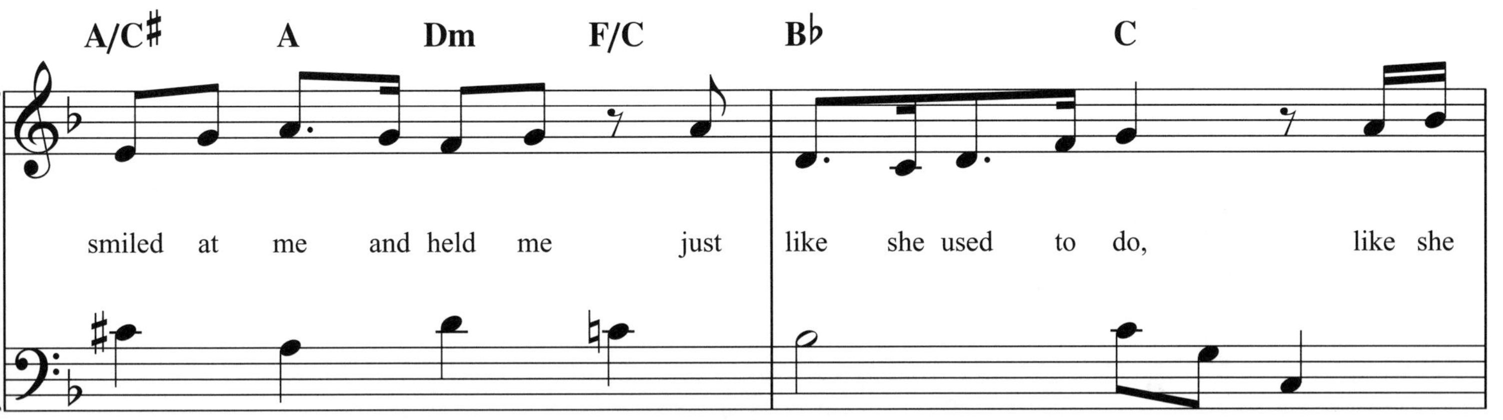
A/C♯
A
Dm
F/C
B♭
C
smiled at me and held me just like she used to do, like she

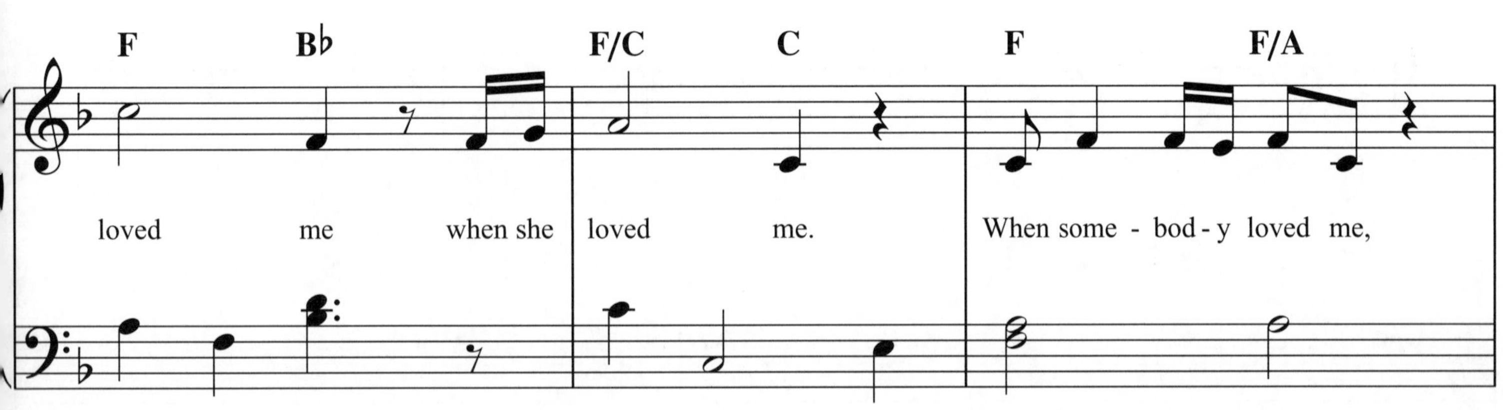
F
B♭
F/C
C
F
F/A
loved me when she loved me. When some - bod - y loved me,

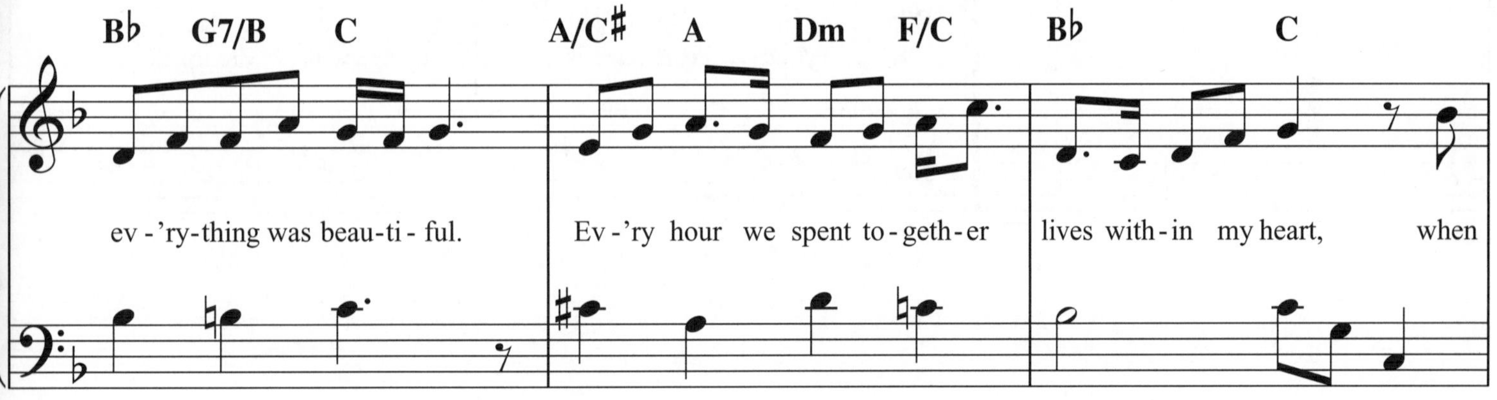
B♭
G7/B
C
A/C♯
A
Dm
F/C
B♭
C
ev - 'ry-thing was beau-ti - ful. Ev - 'ry hour we spent to-geth-er lives with-in my heart, when

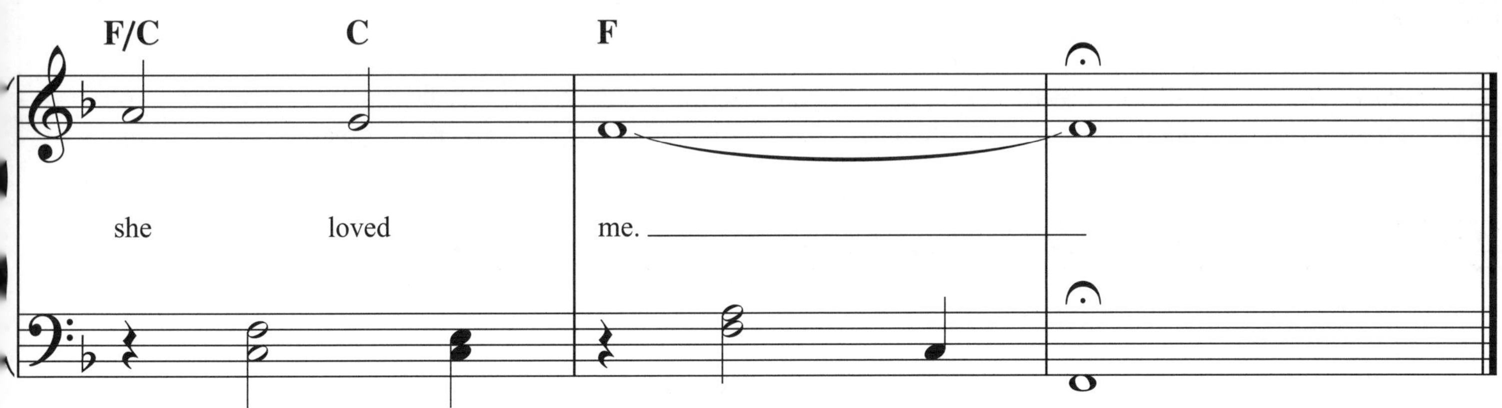
F/C
C
F
she loved me.

WHEN YOU WISH UPON A STAR

from PINOCCHIO

Words by NED WASHINGTON
Music by LEIGH HARLINE

With expression

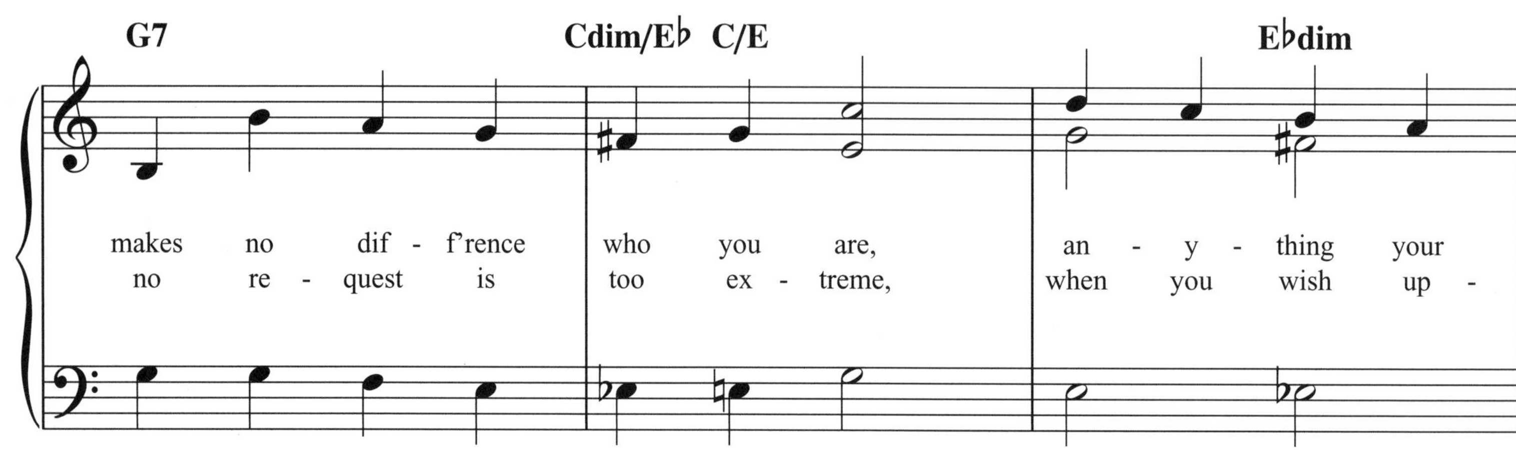

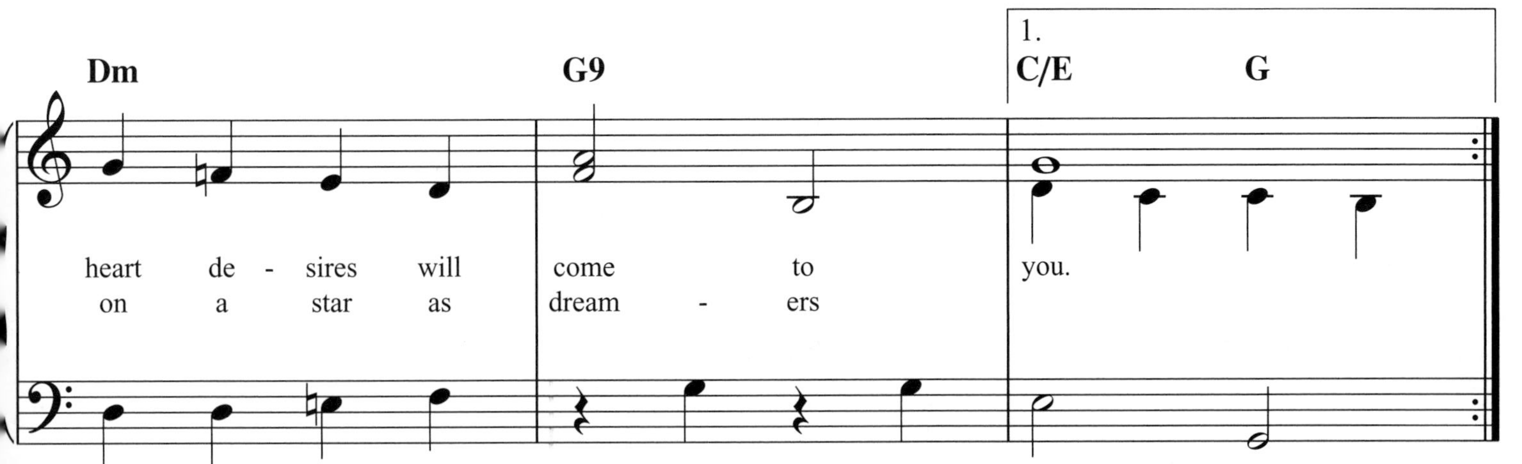
1.
Dm
G9
C/E
G
heart de - sires will come to you.
on a star as dream - ers

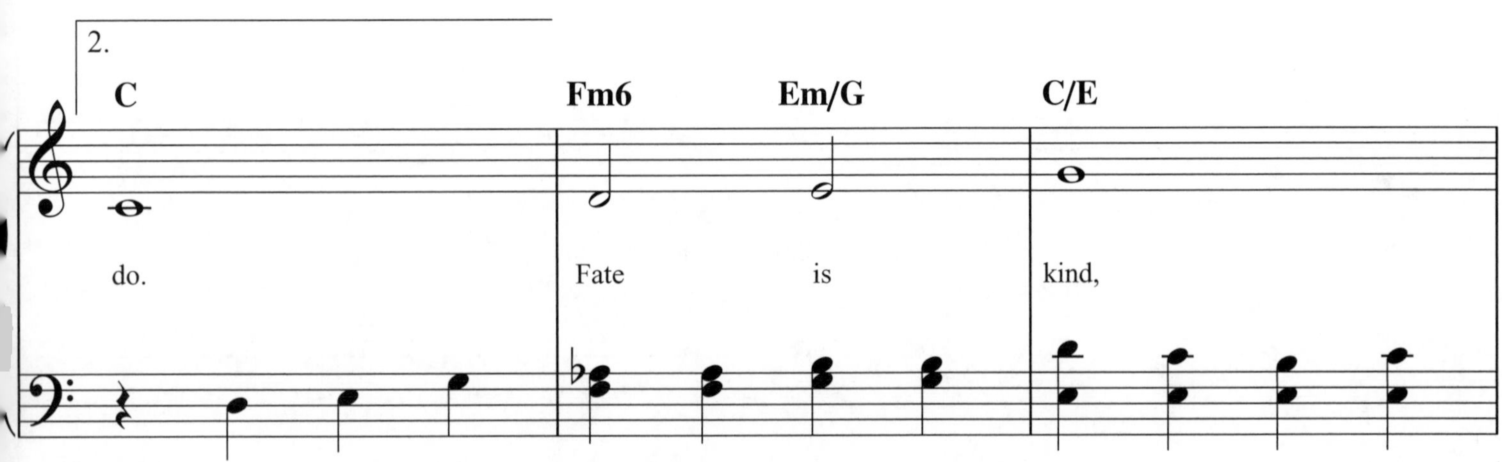
2.
C
Fm6
Em/G
C/E
do. Fate is kind,

Dm/G
Gm
G7/D
Cdim7/E♭
C/E
she brings to those who love

Am
D7/F♯
the sweet ful - fill - ment of their se - cret

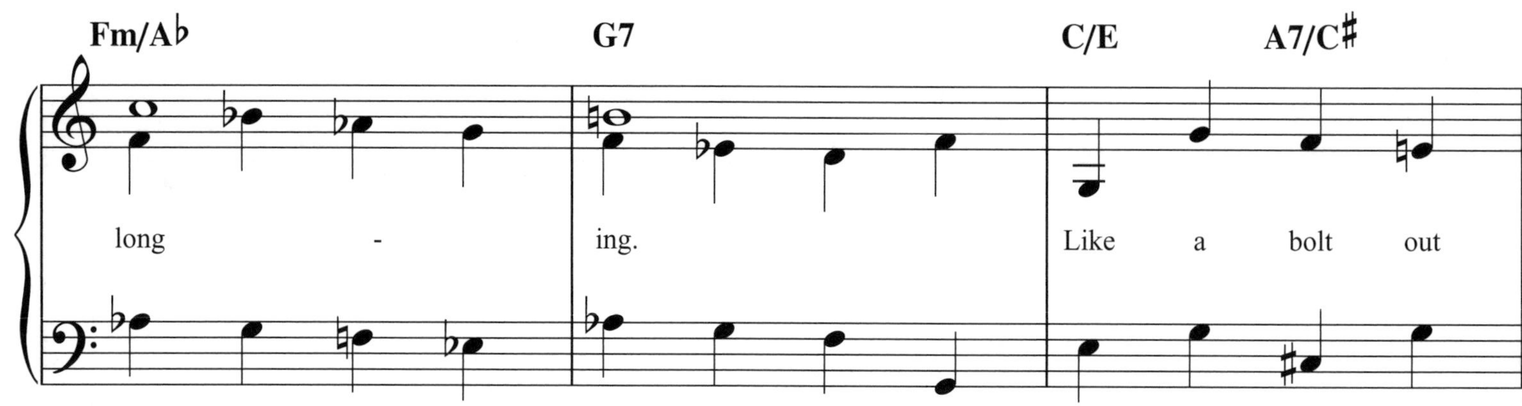
Fm/A♭
G7
C/E
A7/C♯
long - ing.
Like a bolt out

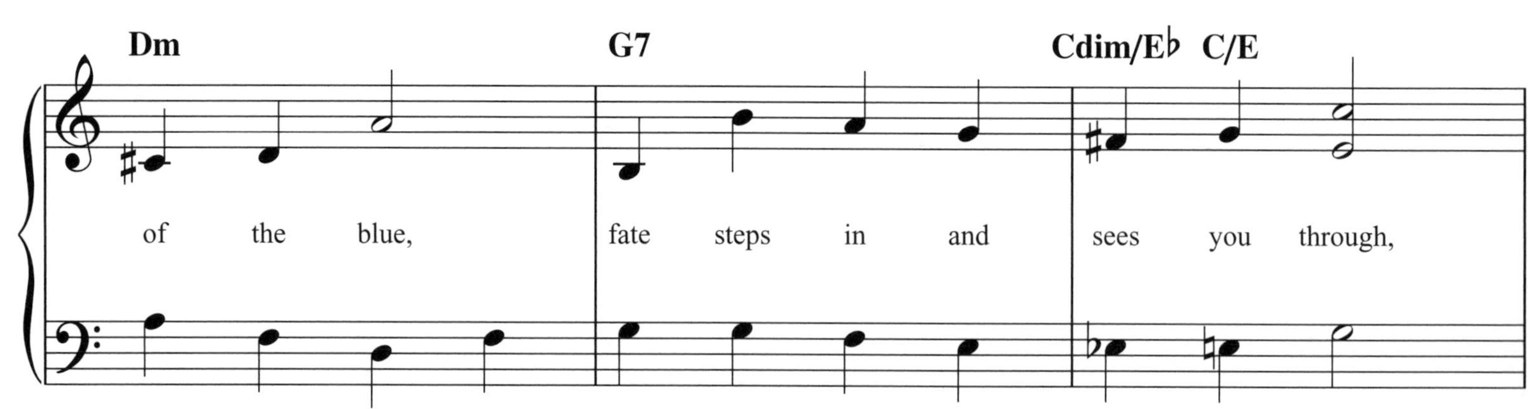
Dm
G7
Cdim/E♭
C/E
of the blue,
fate steps in and
sees you through,

E♭dim
Dm
G9
when you wish up - on a star, your
dream comes

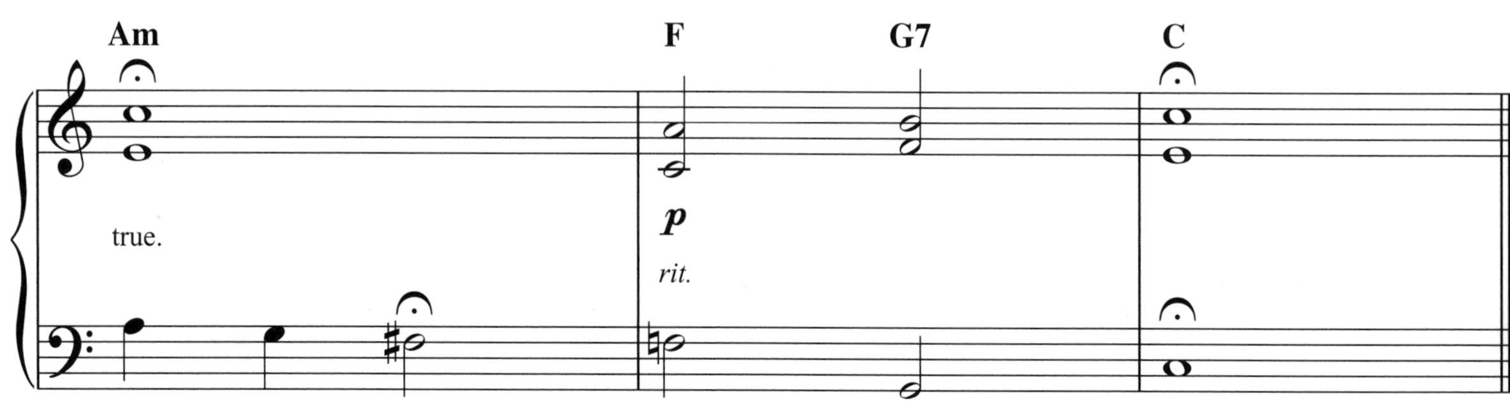
Am
F
G7
C
true.
p
rit.

A WHOLE NEW WORLD

(Aladdin's Theme)
from ALADDIN

Music by ALAN MENKEN
Lyrics by TIM RICE

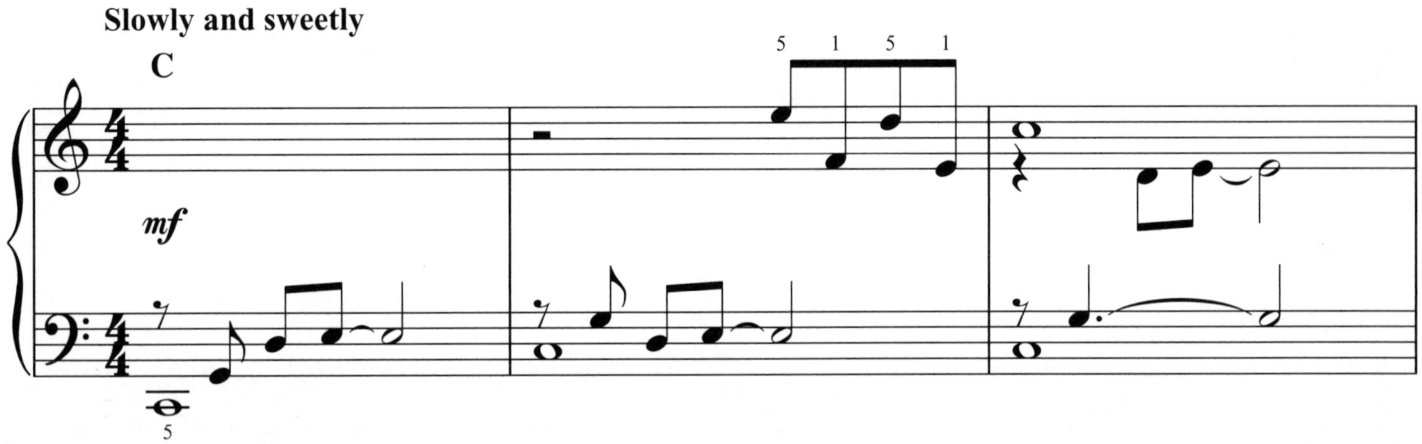

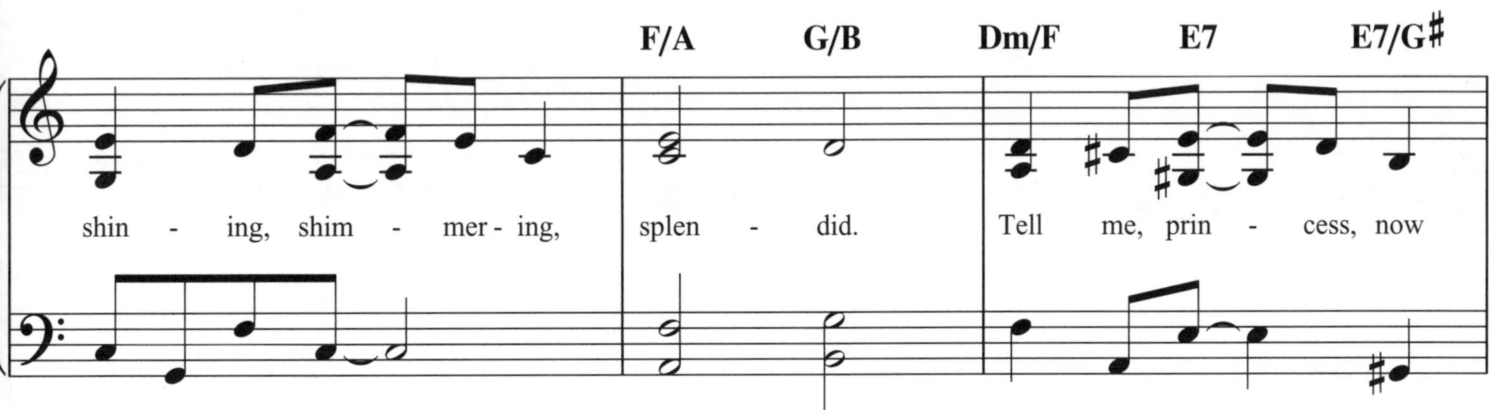

Am Am/G F C G
when did you last let your heart de - cide?

C
I can o - pen your eyes, take you won - der by

F/A G/B Dm/F E7 E7/G♯ Am Am/G
won - der o - ver, side - ways, and un - der on a

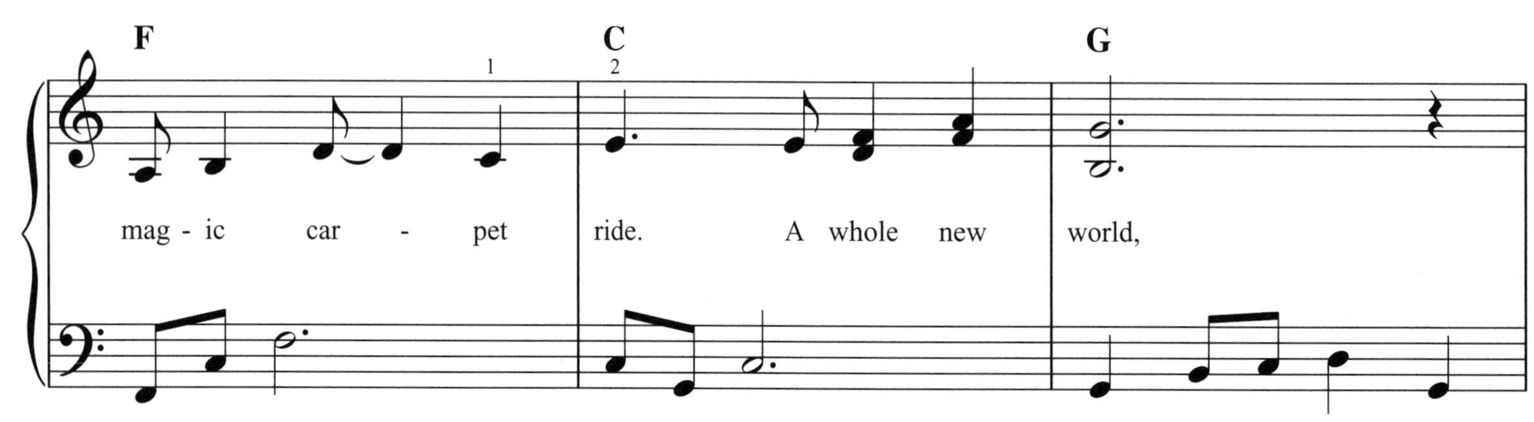
F C G
mag - ic car - pet ride. A whole new world,

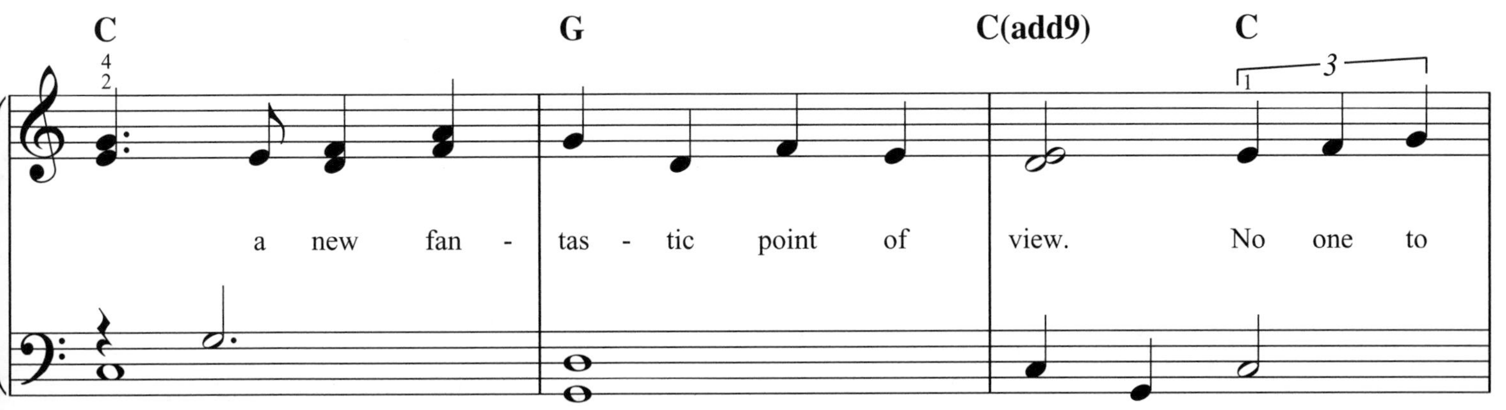
C
G
C(add9)
C
a new fan - tas - tic point of view. No one to

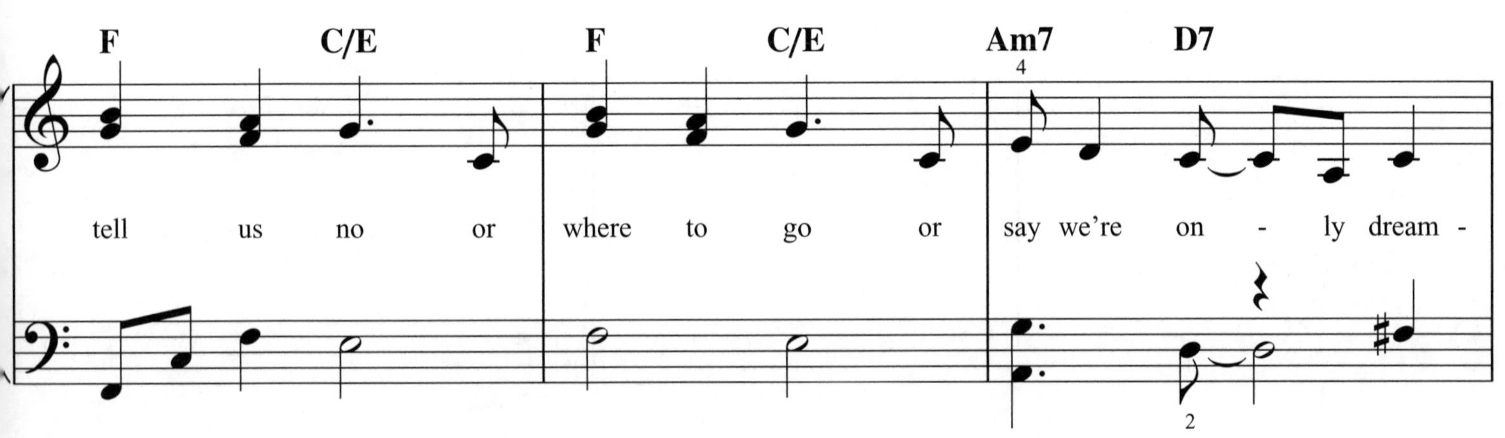
F
C/E
F
C/E
Am7
D7
tell us no or where to go or say we're on - ly dream -

F/G
G
C
ing. A whole new world, a daz - zling

G
G♯dim
Am
C7/B♭
F
C/E
place I nev - er knew. But when I'm way up here it's

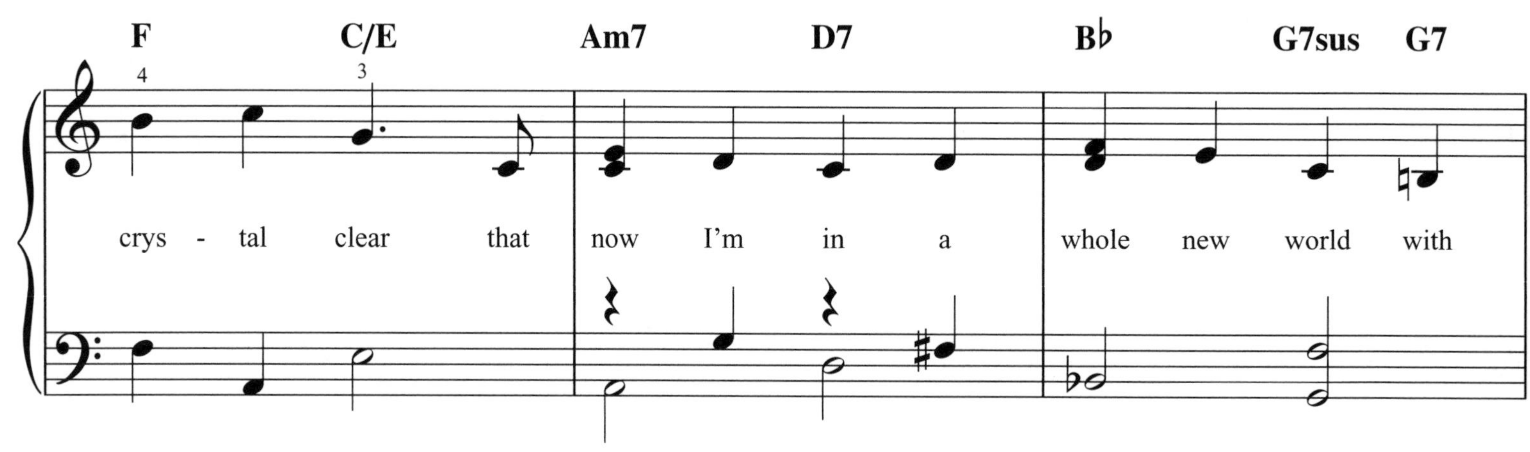
F
C/E
Am7
D7
B♭
G7sus
G7
4
3
crys - tal clear that
now I'm in a
whole new world with

C
F
3
you.
Un - be - liev - a - ble

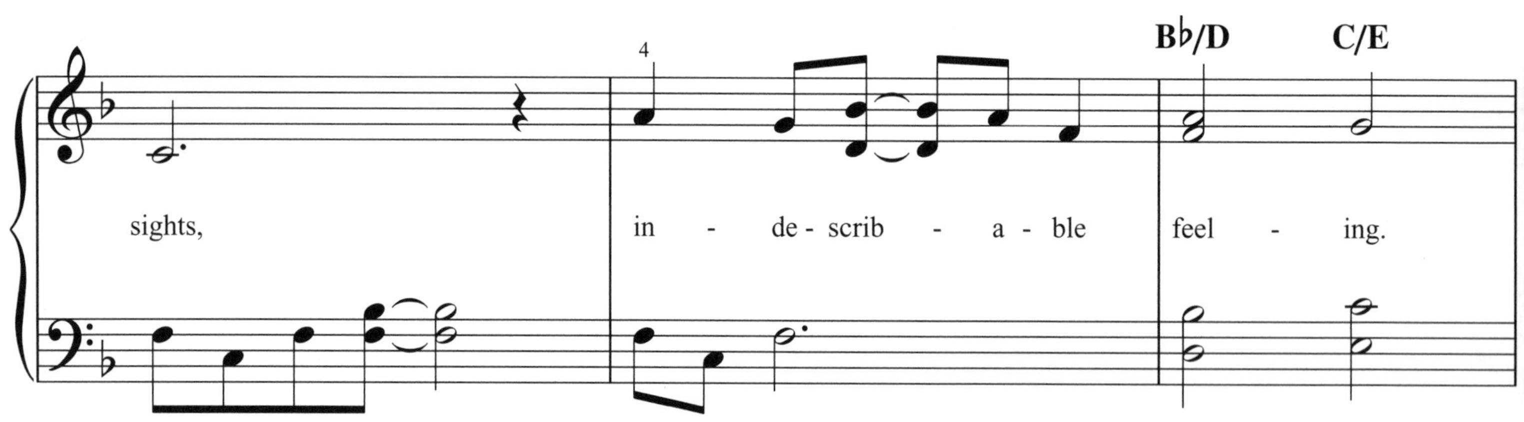
B♭/D
C/E
4
sights,
in - de - scrib - a - ble
feel - ing.

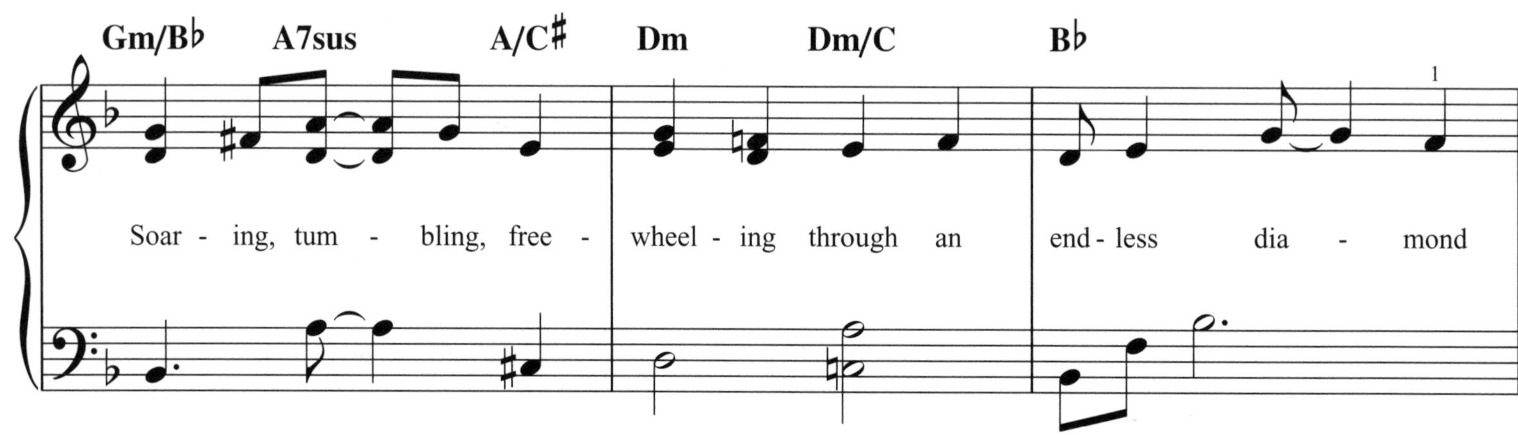
Gm/B♭
A7sus
A/C♯
Dm
Dm/C
B♭
1
Soar - ing, tum - bling, free -
wheel - ing through an
end - less dia - mond

F
C
3
F
2
sky. A whole new
world,
a hun - dred
C
F
3
thou - sand things to
see. I'm like a
B♭
F/A
B♭
F/A
shoot - ing star. I've
come so far I
Dm7
G7sus
G
B♭/C
can't go back to
where I used to

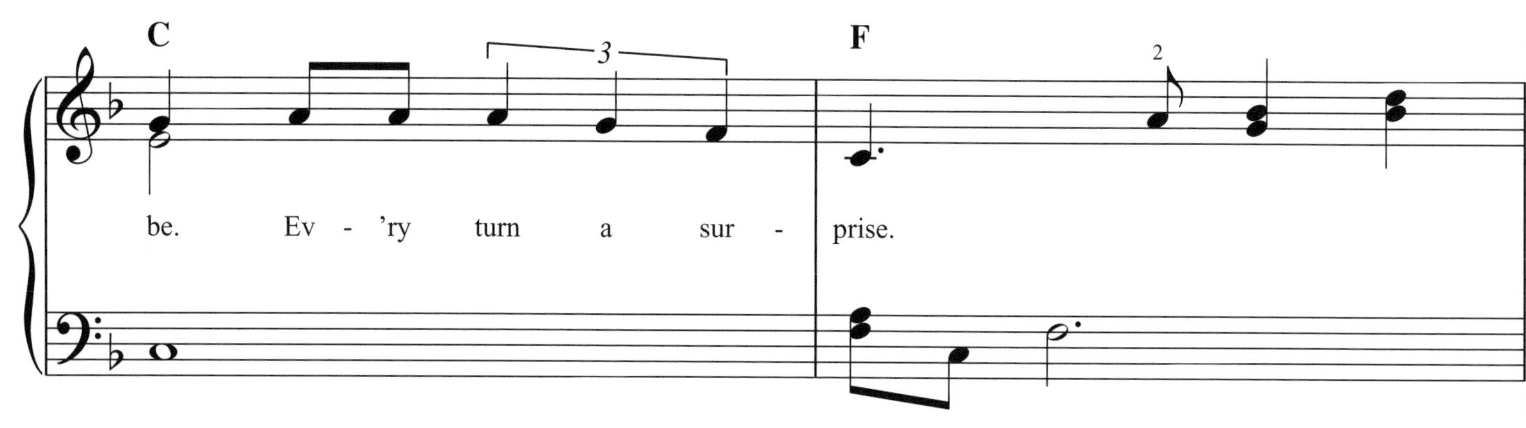
C
F
be. Ev - 'ry turn a sur - prise.

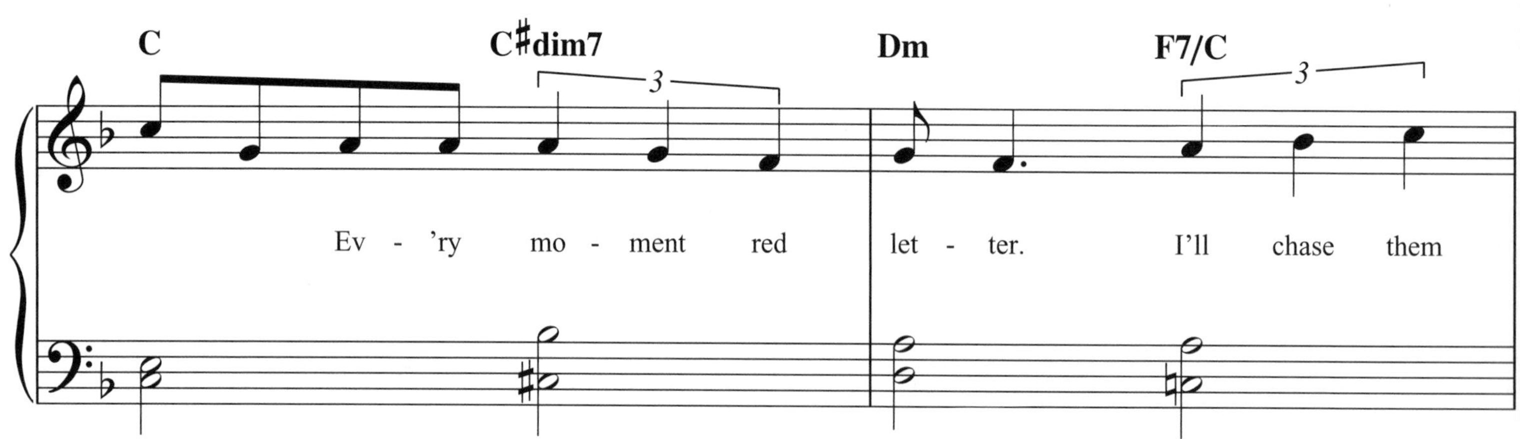
C
C♯dim7
Dm
F7/C
Ev - 'ry mo - ment red let - ter. I'll chase them

B♭
F/A
B♭
F/A
an - y - where. There's time to spare.

Dm7
G7
E♭
C7
Dm
Let me share this whole new world with you.

F/C
B♭
F/A
A whole new
world, a whole new
world, that's where we'll

Gm7
F/A
B♭
be, that's where we'll
be. A thrill - ing
chase, a won - d'rous

C7sus
F
place for you and
me.
5

rit.
2

YOU'LL BE IN MY HEART

from TARZAN™

Words and Music by
PHIL COLLINS

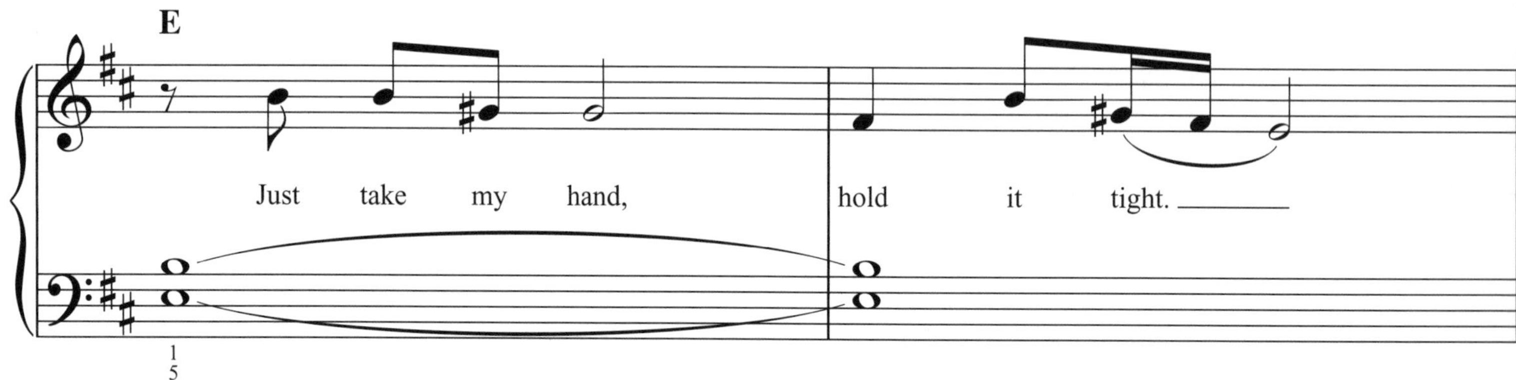

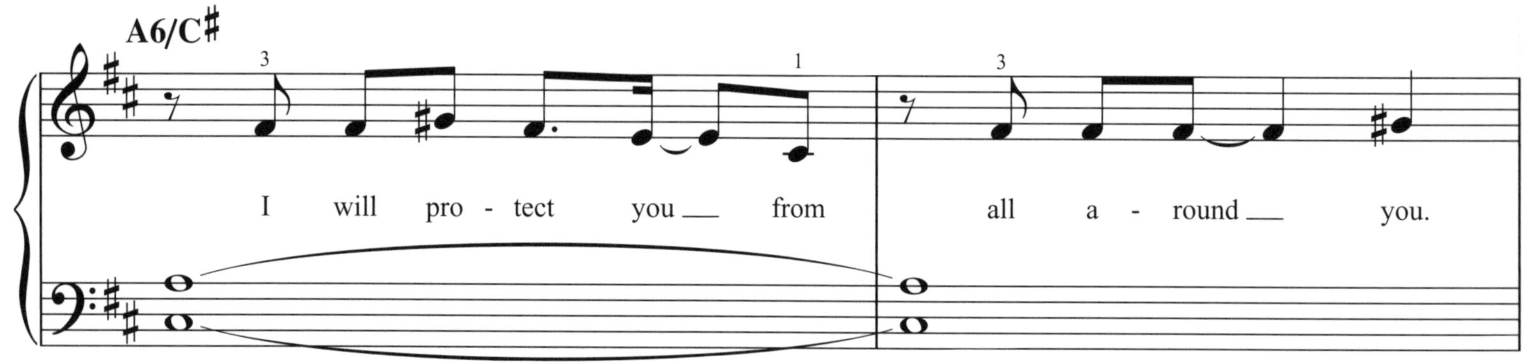

C
F
F/C
C/E
F
seem so strong. _
My arms will hold you, keep you
safe and warm. _

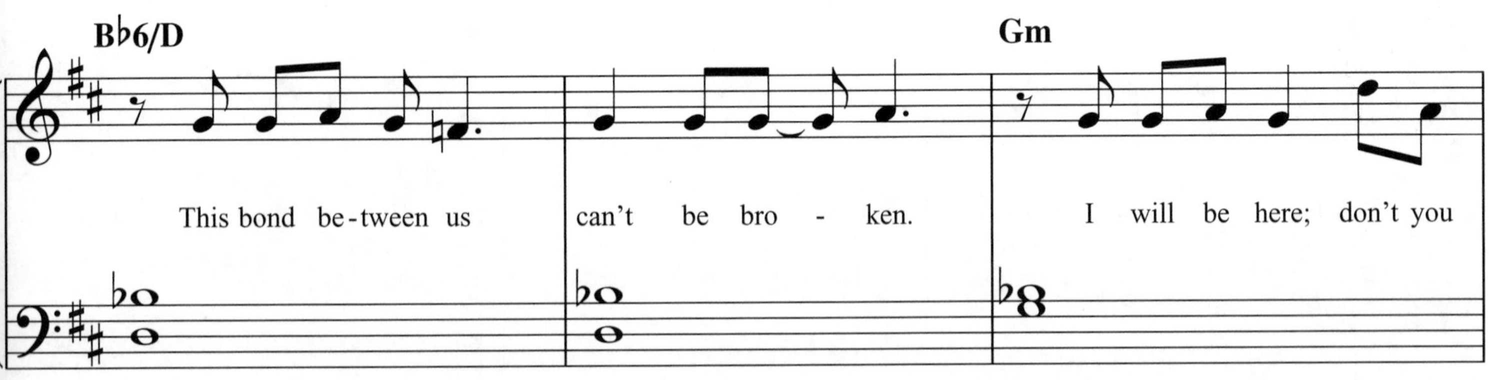
B♭6/D
Gm
This bond be-tween us
can't be bro - ken.
I will be here; don't you

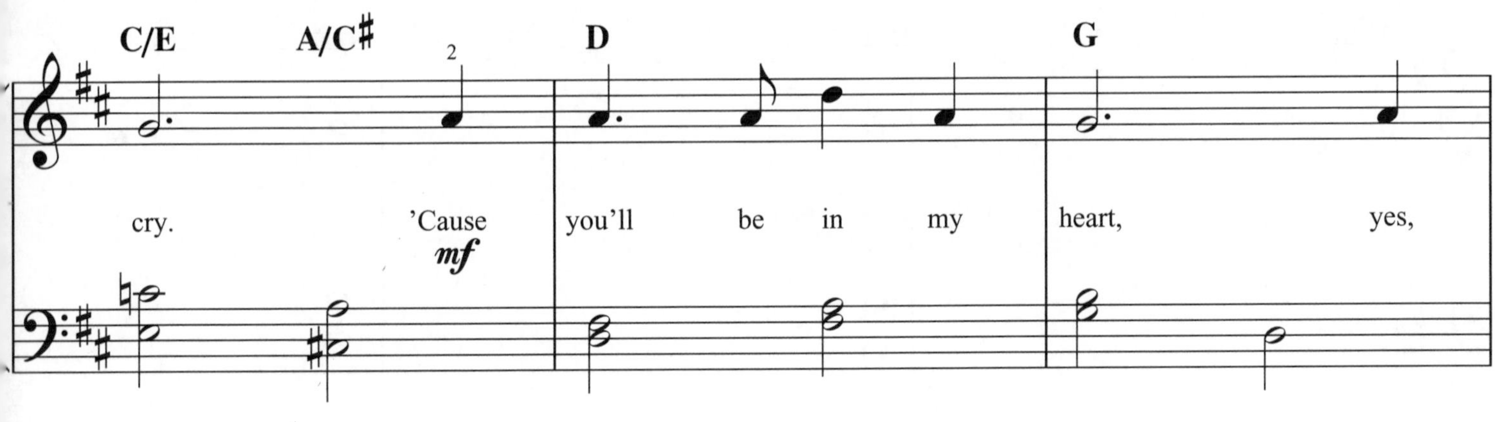
C/E
A/C♯
D
G
cry.
'Cause
mf
you'll be in my
heart, yes,

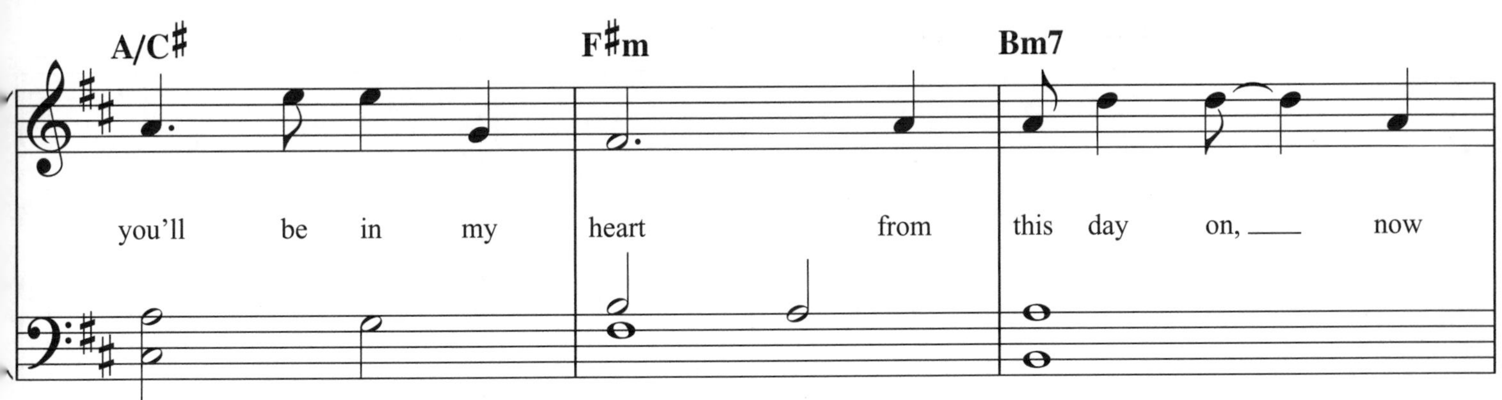
A/C♯
F♯m
Bm7
you'll be in my
heart from
this day on, ___ now

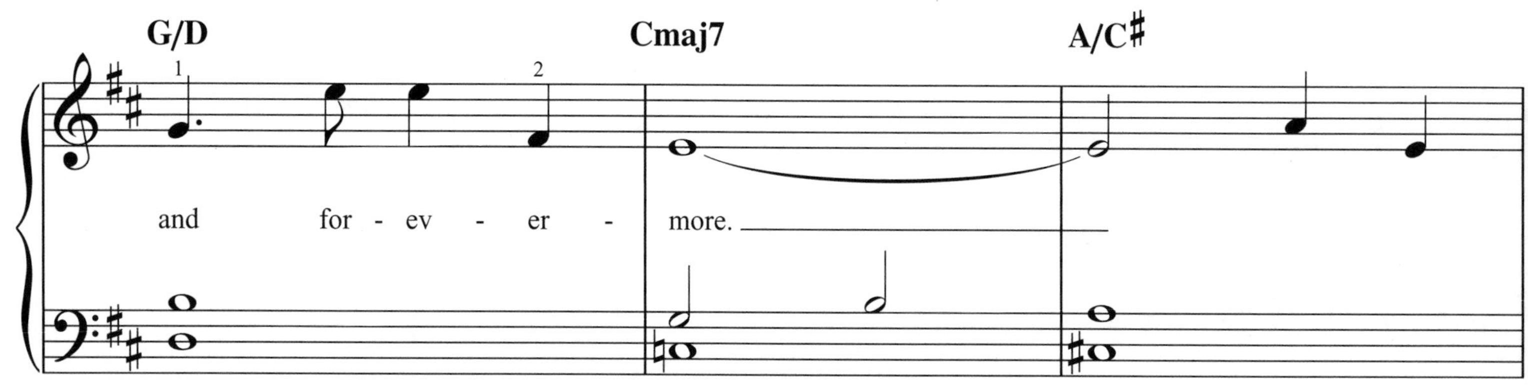
G/D
Cmaj7
A/C♯
and for - ev - er - more.

D
G
A/C♯
You'll be in my heart no mat - ter what they

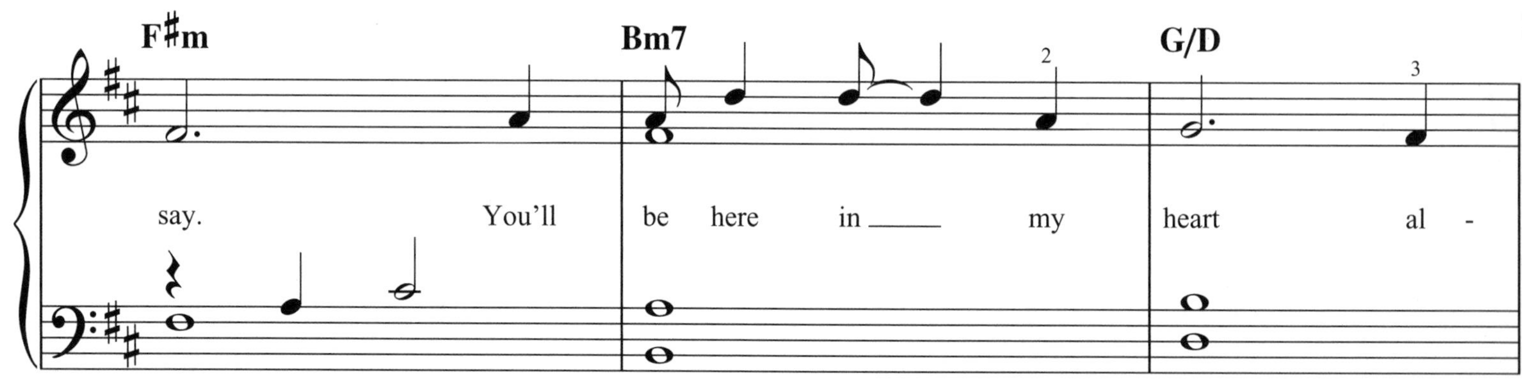
F♯m
Bm7
G/D
say. You'll be here in my heart al -

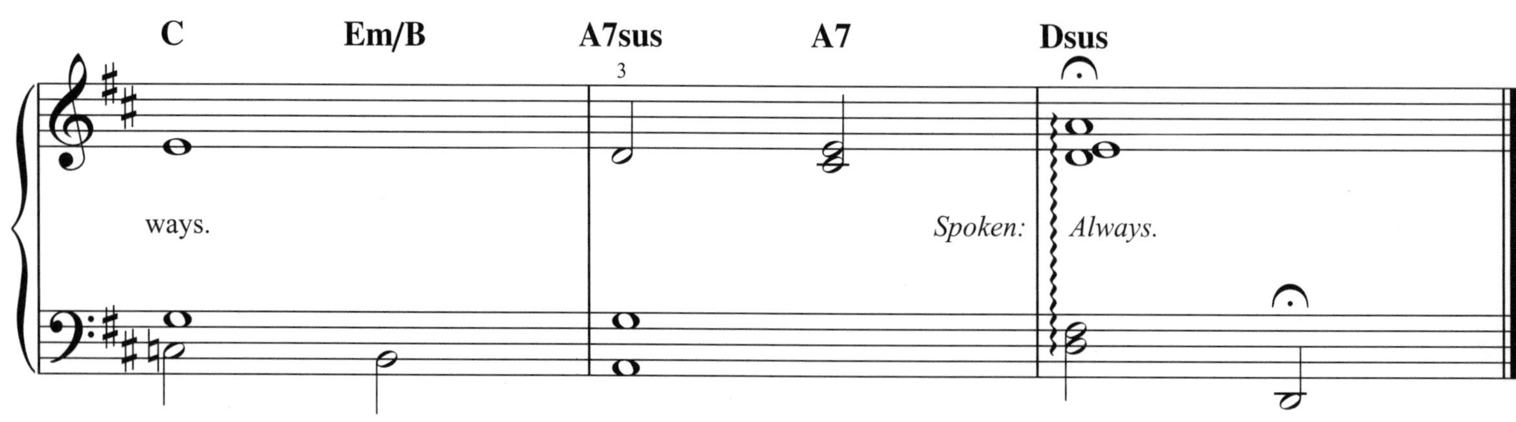
C
Em/B
A7sus
A7
Dsus
ways.
Spoken: Always.